Necessary Wisdom

NECESSARY WISDOM

Jacob Needleman

*Talks About God, Time, Money,
Love, and the Need for
Philosophy*

IN CONVERSATIONS WITH

D. Patrick Miller

FIRST EDITION

Copyright © 2013 by Fearless Books

PO Box 4199 ◆ Napa CA 94558

info@fearlessbooks.com

ISBN: 978-098880240-7

Library of Congress Control Number:
2013931316

Front Cover Photography,
Book Design & Typography:
D. Patrick Miller

Back Cover Photo:
Sari Friedman

CONTENTS

Introduction

Always the beautiful answer
who asks a more beautiful question
— e.e. cummings

WHEN I was twenty, a smart girlfriend who had her hands full saving my sanity gave me a paperback and said, "Here, read this." The book was philosopher Jacob Needleman's THE NEW RELIGIONS, and therein I found a passage that has come to mind periodically ever since. As I've struggled and slept along a faintly marked trail between the devil and the deep blue sea — or what I like to call my "spiritual path"— this paragraph has served me well as a sort of recurring signpost. In discussing the central crisis of Western religion, Needleman wrote:

> It is as though millions of people suffering from a painful disease were to gather together to hear someone read a textbook of medical treatment in which the means necessary to cure their disease were carefully spelled out. It is as though they were all to take great comfort in that book and what they heard, going through their

I

lives knowing that their disease could be cured, quoting passages to their friends, preaching the wonders of this great book, and returning to their congregation from time to time to hear more of the inspiring diagnosis and treatment read to them. Meanwhile, of course, the disease worsens and they eventually die of it, smiling in grateful hope as on their deathbed someone reads to them yet another passage from the text. Perhaps for some a troubling thought crosses their minds as their eyes close for the last time: "Haven't I forgotten something? Something important? Haven't I forgotten to undergo treatment?"

With the additional retrospect of thirty-odd years, my appreciation of this insight has only increased. The author's observation applies not only to the use and misuse of the Bible, but also describes how the followers of any spiritual tradition can fail to implement the teachings of their path. Since THE NEW RELIGIONS was published in 1970, we have seen the dramatic spread and popularization of such alternative spiritual philosophies as Zen Buddhism, Sufism, Kabbalism, and *A Course in Miracles* (ACIM), but it remains to be seen whether Western culture is any closer to curing its "disease" as a result.

In fact, it could be said that the West suffers primarily from a malady that it doesn't even recognize. From day to day, we may think that our worst disease is violence, racism and prejudice, environmental degradation, warfare between nations or cultures, or even physical illnesses such as cancer. But most of these ills could be ameliorated, and some perhaps even eradicated, by *the reclamation and exploration of our inner life.*

The materialistic attitudes of the West — which by now are globally pervasive — tend to discourage even the *recognition* of an inner life. We increasingly believe that our consciousness stems entirely from biochemical reactions in the brain, and that the answers to all our problems will eventually be found in scientific research and technological development. Yet even as science and technology progress, producing remarkable and sometimes dangerous changes in our lifestyles at an ever-increasing pace, the deeper problems of human culture remain: alienation, despair, enmity and misunderstanding, and a fundamental loneliness that separates people from each other in both intimate and social realms.

Human beings have traditionally turned to religion to deal with these deeper problems. But most mainstream religions have become so weighted with superstition, dogma, and recruitment strategies that they often end up exacerbating the human predicament rather than easing it. What's been largely lost in our conventional religious traditions is the understanding that, as Jacob Needleman suggested decades ago, the great spiritual teachings are meant to be *textbooks* for the application of wisdom to our experience in this world. Instead, we tend to treat our books of wisdom as anthologies of beliefs that we merely venerate, or parrot, or rebel against, instead of practical guidebooks that we actually use to explore the territory of our inner lives.

Fortunately, you don't need a mainstream religion to discover or explore your inner life. A great gift of newer spiritual paths like Zen and ACIM is that they have reintroduced to Westerners the concept of a "spiritual discipline" that trains the mind to awaken to spiritual reality. By that, I mean *the deep engagement of our personal consciousness with the nature of consciousness itself.* This is not a scientific or rational process, and its goal is not a refined knowledge, a particular set of beliefs, or a special way of behaving. For lack of better terms by which to describe the indescribable, the spiritual goal is a more alert, more compassionate, and more authentic state of being than most of us would normally develop without a discipline.

When the classic Zen koan asks, "What did your face look like before your parents were born?" it is invoking a questioning stillness that leads not to a logical answer, but to the direct experience of a deeper reality than our thinking mind can usually grasp. When the Course asserts, *"Nothing real can be threatened. Nothing unreal exists. Herein lies the peace of God"* it is pointing toward the same mystical awareness.

A spiritual discipline that many people are not aware of is the practice of philosophy. For most, philosophy may well mean a dry-bones collection of hoary old ideas once written about by a bunch of dead guys. We may have brushed up against Philosophy 101 in college as a throwaway elective; we may even pay lip service to the contributions of such iconic figures as Socrates, Plato, Kierkegaard, or Kant. But not many of us could even briefly summarize what such teachers had to say, or what relevance they might have to our everyday lives.

Among living philosophers, Jacob Needleman stands out for his lifelong dedication to bringing his discipline out of the academic lecture hall and into the everyday lives of his students and the readers of his best-selling books. While he can knowledgeably discuss the contributions of all the great philosophers and the various traditions they represent, he has always been more interested in helping ordinary people become their own philosophers. In his view, an effective philosopher is not someone who formulates "final answers" to the great questions of human existence, but someone who constantly asks questions in order to raise new ideas that, in turn, provoke deeper and greater questions. It is exactly this ever-progressive questioning and testing of ideas that lies at the heart of genuine spiritual development — and that may lead us, in ways we cannot rationally plan or predict, to the healing of the greatest human problems.

BORN in Philadelphia and raised in a Jewish intellectual environment in which "becoming a doctor was the only human thing to do," Jacob Needleman entered Harvard University with the intention of going on to medical school. But then something went awry, as the young student's obsessions with the "big questions" of life steered him into the pursuit of philosophy.

"My father never understood what I was doing," Needleman recalls, and his mother didn't take his decision well either. When the newly-minted Ph.D. (from Yale) was first introduced socially as "Dr. Needleman" in her presence, she joked, "He's not the kind of doctor that does anybody any good, you know."

Dr. Needleman has never been what an academic philosopher is supposed to be, either. Early on, he departed from the soulless pursuit of argumentative logic and analysis to teach and write at the "heart of philosophy," dealing with those "Why am I here?" questions that inexorably cross over into the academically suspect realm of spirituality. At Harvard he was the only student to sign up for an esoteric course on Vedanta, and in ensuing years he studied Zen and the other westward-drifting Eastern traditions. He also encountered the teachings of the Russian mystic G.I. Gurdjieff, which remain a touchstone of his perspective.

Needleman has spent five decades as a professor at San Francisco State University, with some sabbaticals to write or edit books on consciousness and spirituality, including such landmark works as THE HEART OF PHILOSOPHY, LOST CHRISTIANITY, MONEY AND THE MEANING OF LIFE, THE AMERICAN SOUL and, in 2010, WHAT IS GOD? When I met him for our first interview in the late 1980s, I had been following the work of Dr. Needleman for about fifteen years and already considered him my chief mentor in my studies of spirituality.

By that time I had abandoned my early interest in investigative reporting and, having taken over the task of saving my own sanity, was just beginning a career that I eventually labeled the "journalism of consciousness." I was fortunate to find an editor, Sy Safransky, who shared this interest, and his magazine *The Sun*, published in Chapel Hill, N.C., would eventually publish three of the six pieces collected here. Another was featured on my own website over a decade ago, and two were conducted exclusively for publication in this book.

Thus this volume represents my longest-running "feature story" in the journalism of consciousness, and it's especially gratifying to summarize here my role as the most frequent published interviewer of Dr. Needleman over the course of his fascinating career. His books have much more to say than this brief volume, of course, and I highly recommend that interested readers start with any one of them and keep reading through the Needleman oeuvre. (A complete bibliography of his works appears at the end of this book.)

From this collection of talks, however, you should be able to grasp his fundamental approach to the "big questions" that concern us all, as well as enjoying some intriguing views of the six major topics we have tackled together: **Making Sense of Mysticism, The Secrets of Time and Love, The Meanings of Money, Searching for the Soul of America, Meeting God Without Religion,** and finally, **The Need for Philosophy.** I've written a short introduction for each interview; thereafter my questions appear in italics and Dr. Needleman's answers are in roman, following his initials.

One thing you cannot easily discern from these printed conversations is the face-to-face experience of sharing philosophical inquiries with Jacob Needleman. Unlike political pundits with prepared sound-bites or gurus with mystical aphorisms, this philosopher is often content *not* to have an answer at the ready. In fact, there have been many times when his first response to an inquiry has been, "Hmm, that's an interesting question. Can I take a little while to think about that?" Then a minute or two of silence will ensue while he goes silent and appears to actually search his mind for a novel response.

In those times of intense quiet, I always get the distinct sensation that the actual practice of philosophy is going on between us. This kind of philosophy involves the deep consideration of a question, not with the aim of producing a perfectly phrased answer, but with a focus on the search for truth. It's that very searching which provides the kind of answer we need for so many of our most challenging questions about life, love, and how to conduct ourselves through our short life spans on this earth. There is no single, infallible philosophy that can provide all the answers for human beings in the infinitely various circumstances of our lives. But by learning to reconnect our inner life with our everyday thoughts, beliefs, and behaviors, we can all engage in the deep questioning that ultimately provides us with the moment-by-moment instincts of a necessary wisdom.

Making Sense of Mysticism

W HEN the following interview was first published in *The Sun* in 1989, the so-called "New Age" was in full swing. A loose amalgam of social movements involving alternative health approaches, natural foods, Eastern spiritual influences, Western esotericism, and old-time snake-oil hucksterism, the New Age had some obvious roots in the counterculture that arose in the mid-60s. By the turn of the new millennium, the New Age was no longer recognized as a distinct cultural phenomenon. But that's largely because many of its most significant innovations had been integrated into society, and were thus no longer "countercultural."

Yoga and meditation, formerly fringe practices known to relatively few Westerners as recently as the 70s, are now widely practiced in schools, fitness centers, and corporate gyms. Acupuncture, naturopathy, and other "complementary" medical approaches enjoy widespread popular acceptance, if not mainstream medical approval. Natural and organic foods have a section devoted to them in virtually every grocery store, not to mention the presence of the hugely successful Whole Foods Market chain across the US. And many people now have at least a passing familiarity with some mystical principles of Zen, Vedanta, Kabbalism, traditional shamanism, and other "alternative" spiritual paths that often have deeper historical roots than contemporary Christianity. The fact that 30% of adult Americans — and up to 70% of the young Millennial generation — now identify themselves as "spiritual but not religious" owes much to the integration of a New Age perspective in the American popular consciousness.

But as writer Mitch Horowitz reveals in his excellent book OCCULT AMERICA: *The Secret History of How Mysticism Shaped Our Nation*, the spiritual side of the New Age wasn't really new, but rather the cyclical reappearance of a strain of mystical thought that has always been part of American consciousness. What's most interesting about the recent recurrence of American mysticism is that it has arisen in the midst of a scientific and highly technological age. This creates a novel tension around the issues of mystical thought and practice — and some novel ways of misunderstanding the authentic use of "esoteric" (meaning *inner*) practices. Jacob Needleman was looking seriously at the most recent reawakening of American mysticism well before it was noticed by most observers, and the following conversation reveals some of his key insights.

Since you wrote THE NEW RELIGIONS *in 1970, how has their popular spread in the West affected our spiritual condition? Are we any closer to "undergoing treatment" for our underlying ills?*

JN: I think some people are. The idea of that passage [quoted in the Introduction] was that every religion offers an inner practice, as well as a doctrine of morality and theology. That practical method is the original core of any religion, and it offers a means for allowing a teaching to enter into one's body, life, and everyday actions. In the West, that inner practice has often been forgotten; we've been satisfied with religious doctrine. The new religions that have come to us have introduced many people to core practices.

But there's always the question of what really constitutes the "treatment." Not all things that present themselves as practices are genuine. A spiritual method can easily become just another idea to be talked about but not undertaken.

How do you feel about the ideas and practices generally labeled as New Age?

JN: I think anybody with any sense will admit that it's a huge mixed bag. There are some very hopeful and interesting things going on within the New Age, and there's a lot of nonsense, fraudulence, and wishful thinking. But I think that's always the price paid for the rise of a valuable new idea. Something powerful will always be surrounded by many levels of phenomena that are not as intense or authentic as the core. At the lowest level, you'll have absolute rubbish, and there's plenty of that in the New Age.

In the United States, it seems that even a new spirituality has to come to us through capitalism — that is, almost all our information is marketed in one way or another. To me, one of the biggest problems of the New Age is its marketing of spirituality. Money pervades everything in our society.

JN: So does advertising, which is driven by the intent to sell and persuade. An authentic spiritual path doesn't persuade; it simply makes itself known. When advertising and spirituality get mixed up, it's hard to separate the functions of communication and persuasion. Anyone involved with real spirituality in this society has to work very hard just to understand how to communicate without becoming trapped by marketing.

Behind this problem is the old and very good question for human beings: How to be in the world but not of the world? To avoid pollution of your work, you have to discriminate, and develop your own feeling for where the line is drawn on the issue of "selling out." Not all selling is selling out.

There's a story of a king who ruled a country where the water was poisoned. The poison made people insane, but the king had pure water brought to him. Gradually he came to realize that he wasn't able to rule his country because he wasn't crazy; he couldn't understand his people. So he had just enough of the poisoned water mixed in his own to make him a little crazy. Then he could rule more effectively.

What's "out there" is "in here," too. You have to know what's out there as well as what's inside you. It's a major question for all of us: How do you engage honestly with the world as it is, and how do you know when you're selling out?

David Ogilvy founded one of the world's most successful ad agencies with the guideline, "Tell the truth." He gave up the Rolls Royce account because he decided their cars weren't living up to his advertising...

JN: And how much money did he have by that time?

Well, by the time you can give up the Rolls Royce account you don't have to worry about sacrificing everything for truth. But his message was that truth sells. I'm not sure I believe him.

JN: During the many years I've observed businesses, I've seen that the ones which succeed have something resembling integrity, even if you wouldn't call it a spiritual integrity. It's something that works at the level where people want to trust. People feel so alone.

Eastern teachers in this country seem to have suffered from that kind of isolation: they have a lot of followers, but few friends. I've always felt that what undid Bhagwan Shree Rajneesh (known posthumously as Osho) in America was the loss of his peers. After a while there was no one who could say to him, "Aren't ten Rolls-Royces enough, my friend?"

JN: Yes, in this culture you just can't go it alone as a teacher. You need the correctives of a group or community of equals. The original forms of Eastern practice had a lot of checks and balances to keep people from going off the deep end. Some Eastern teachers have certainly been taken in by our cult of the individual. But Western monastic traditions guard against this tendency also. You always have "the brethren" to deal with. The temptation to go it alone can easily become a temptation to be "the one," for any kind of teacher.

What is the difference between conventional religion and the inner practice that you spoke of?

JN: Christianity, Judaism, and Islamic belief all provide people with moral precepts, that is, ways of living meant to be obeyed by the masses. Any such way of living is based on a particular vision of human nature and society, and is intended to give balance and steadiness to our experience. But it's not really intended to *transform* us, to give us nirvana or God-realization. If kept authentically, a traditional religion can bring a few people who are seeking more to "the path" in relatively good shape. Their psyches are not torn apart or so terribly neurotic. This is the point of the exoteric function of the great religions — what Islam calls the *shariat*, its laws, customs, and traditions. It's a very important part of balancing human life. At their best these rules help us manage our affairs with compassion for each other.

Within the *shariat* is the *tarikat*: the way or the path. In Islam, this esoteric function is embodied by the Sufis, among others. Many great teachers have said that the esoteric work is only for those who have been through the exoteric, and have achieved the necessary balance. It's true that the message of the great esoteric traditions is that only an inner change can genuinely infuse outer actions with truth, love, and power. But most of these transformative techniques were intended for people who had lived in balance within a tradition. What we're getting recently in the West is a lot of information about inner practice, available to people who haven't had much of an outer practice.

That brings up an interesting question: Are these methods going to be wasted, or even have a destructive effect on people whose outer, everyday lives are in great imbalance?

It also brings up the question of whether we have any choice now.

JN: That's right. When the question unfolds, we realize we have no choice: it's too late for a new morality to be imposed. So we're faced with the problem of levels — how to recognize when a particular idea or practice is too much for us. If a spiritual practice is too intense, it "blows your mind" and becomes overly fascinating, or leads you into fantasy. You could compare the esoteric core of a religion to a pure, high-octane fuel. Put it into an old Volkswagen, and the car will go like hell for a mile before it blows apart. If we're going to have a spiritual path for our culture, it needs to have levels that recognize where we are, and gradually lead us upward.

Is there any way that people who haven't been following the outer practices of any given tradition can recognize what level of inner work they can handle?

JN: That's generally up to the teacher. So we arrive at the need for authentic teachers, with the requisite vision, wisdom, and insight into human character. A beginner will usually have only the vaguest idea of an appropriate level.

Do you agree with the premise that mysticism without morality produces monsters like Hitler — or that while liberation from ordinary awareness may feel good, it has the potential to do great damage?

JN: This is a question that deserves more discussion than we can give it here. Isolated experiences of extraordinary states of consciousness can be appropriated by the ego with harmful or dangerous results. And, it may be possible that even the attainment of a sustained, higher-level consciousness can be "infected" by something mysteriously dark in human nature — with sometimes horrific results.

But true mystical experience, deriving from sustained and balanced inner work, almost inevitably involves the awakening of feeling of a special kind, a feeling that is intrinsically moral. In this sense, you could not possibly be a true spiritual mystic and end up a monster like Hitler.

Now there are repressed functions within us whose release gives us a distinct liberating pleasure. For someone living an uptight, head-restricted existence, a hot tub can feel extraordinary, but it's not necessarily a mystical experience. Some people live such constricted lives that even the slightest triggering of a new vital energy can mistakenly be labeled "spiritual."

Being fully present to the most mundane thing, like eating some fruit at lunch, *can* be a mystical experience. It's the quality of consciousness that makes the difference. Those who have developed their awareness may have a more mystical experience drinking their morning coffee than an unprepared person would have meditating in a monastery.

So the mystic must have a respect for the mundane.

JN: Well, it's respect for consciousness that matters. The mundane is a part of reality and you respect it for what it is. A chair is not an archangel, but you can be in a state that makes sitting in a chair full of meaning. You might also call it a respect for the present moment.

In Consciousness and Tradition, *you wrote about the tendency to confuse the* process *of consciousness with its* contents *— that is, when we achieve a new level of awareness we can become so fascinated with what we experience at that level that we forget how we got there and stop progressing.*

JN: It's important to remember that today's answer is not

the answer. One always has to rediscover the right response within oneself, and the key is in developing an appreciation for consciousness itself — and to understand how that's different from what we're conscious of. The more you realize what it actually means to be awake, the more alive all your functions will be. New thoughts, new feelings, and new insights come to you, and those can be seductive; so you have to remember that awareness is the vehicle for all of them. That's part of why the great spiritual traditions tell us not to get swept away even if someone like the Buddha appears to us. It's your own consciousness that counts, the Buddha-nature within you.

In THE HEART OF PHILOSOPHY *you wrote about the experience of bringing philosophy to high school students, and the first sentence of the book was, "Man cannot live without philosophy." This reminded me that the "big questions" are always being asked by children, but as adults we tend to regard them as trivial distractions from our real-world concerns. When were you first aware of the big questions, and did you ever lose touch with them?*

JN: I can't remember not being aware of those questions, although I didn't always have them in an intellectual form. As a child I looked at the stars and wondered, "Why am I here? What's going on? Who am I?" I was a semi-prodigy in astronomy, and started reading books on it when I was about five or six. One incident that typified my early frustration had to do with ordering a telescope from a catalogue that advertised the "wonders of science." I saved up my money and ordered the telescope with great excitement, and what I got back was two chintzy little pieces of glass to build a telescope around. That was awfully disappointing. And the more I read in science, the more I felt cheated. One book showed a bird feeding her baby, and the caption said that the mother bird didn't really care about feeding, she was just instinctively responding to the color of the baby bird's throat. That's what made her put the worm in the baby's mouth. I remember thinking, "That can't be right."

These were the first blows I received from the "scientistic" view that nature is blind, mechanical, and without inherent meaning or purpose. That didn't make me forget my big questions, but neither did I swing to the other extreme of a Walt Dis-ney view of nature. I did experience a basic dualism between my firsthand love of nature and the official scientistic view of reality.

At the age of fourteen, I was walking down the street one day and suddenly realized, "I am here. I'm Jerry, and I'm here." It was an extraordinary experience of self-awareness for which there was no support or understanding in school. When I reached college and took my first philosophy course, the instructor asked everyone why they were there — what everyone expected to get from the class — and I said, "I want to know the meaning of life." Everybody started snickering, and the professor said, "If that's what you want, you should see a psychiatrist or a priest. We're here mainly to learn how to think logically and clearly."

In its extreme form, that leads to what I would call metaphysical repression. In our culture, I think metaphysical repression is much more serious than sexual repression. We do not honor the big questions enough, and you literally have to find out about God in the streets, not unlike the way many kids find out about sex. As a youngster, you get your metaphysical information from your buddies. I was fortunate to have family members who respected my questions, and that helped keep them alive for me. But there was no support from the culture.

I entered pre-med because I loved science and nature, and I wanted to be a research biologist. When I saw how happy my parents were that I might be a doctor, my choice seemed confirmed. But then I became discouraged with science in college. I'd read Plato on my own and recognized that my real questions were being taken up there. I felt there was really no other place for me to go.

Can philosophy be unconcerned with spirituality?

JN: No. That's ridiculous. You can call it philosophy, but you'd be mistaking only one branch — that of logic, critical thinking, and analysis — for the whole tree. Philosophy is intrinsically concerned with the search for wisdom, and wisdom means the ability to understand our place in the universe and live in accordance with that understanding. The roots of philosophy are in Plato, Pythagoras, and Aristotle, who were concerned with precisely those questions. The techniques of logical thinking can serve the larger questions, but otherwise they have as much to do with computer science as with philosophy.

Do you think there are any great philosophers in the purely logical mode?

JN: Yes. Wittgenstein, for one. Ludwig Wittgenstein was one of the main sources of the modern Anglo-American style of philosophy, although I believe his thinking has been misunderstood. He generated two major movements of modern philosophy: one is known as logical positivism, and the other as the philosophy of ordinary language. But both of his great visions have been considerably narrowed by some of his followers and critics.. He did have a mystical side, and I regard him as a kind of Zen master before anybody in the West knew about Zen. He had a great feeling for music and silence, and what Kierkegaard called "indirect communication." He had tremendous charismatic power and became something of a celebrity in England, but his personal life was a torment, haunted by the suicides of three brothers.

Recent years have seen people turning to popular philosophers instead of therapists for help in thinking through their personal problems. Do you think that more people are turning to philosophy because our materialism hasn't made us happy?

JN: That's true for some, but I think materialism is still very strong, and more important to many people than they will admit. I'm sorry to give a complicated answer, but I don't think the reaction is that simple. For one thing, mankind has always been screwed up — screwed up in the East, screwed up in the West, screwed up everywhere. Mankind has always been basically a mess. When the Buddha said, "Life is suffering," this was partially an acknowledgment that the world is a difficult place.

Our particular modern hang-up in the West is related to an overemphasis on the intellect, cutting us off from the body and feeling. But all cultures have their imbalances. Throughout history, the great spiritual teachers have adjusted the perennial truths to treat the particular imbalance of a culture in its time. Our disease of the last six or seven hundred years is the tyranny over nature and our bodies, and we're beginning to see through that repression.

On the other hand, Western society is not all bad. We've invented the extraordinary tool known as science, even if we've created some disasters with it. But scientific perception itself is one of the great visions of mankind's history. To adhere to what works — and not be tricked or led only by blind belief — is a very honorable pursuit. Likewise, capitalism is not horrible as an ideal; there's nothing wrong with serving society by making and marketing goods. Not everybody can be a doctor, after all! The great spiritual traditions basically respect businessmen as a necessary part of the human family.

There's no point in blasting away at Western culture indiscriminately, but we have to acknowledge that things have gotten really bad in a certain way. And what's bad has more strength than a lot of New Agers want to admit. To say that we're all turning toward "meaning" is to risk seeing a *Time* cover story on Meaning before very long, and that would be the end of it.

The results of this cultural tendency are pretty hilarious sometimes. There's an old saying that life is a tragedy for the person who feels, and a comedy for the person who thinks. It's funny to see what becomes fashionable in a pseudo-serious way: salt is bad for you, then sugar, then fat. I guess I don't have to tell you that journalism is largely responsible for this rapid succession of fashions in thought. We want constant stimulation, and the press perpetuates that desire. We settle for the most superficial thoughts, taking one look at a situation and then moving on to the next.

In A SENSE OF THE COSMOS, *you recounted the story of a painful illness that brought you to this realization: "When I wish for immortality, I wish for the immortality of my habits." Even when we realize we're being pushed toward a greater consciousness, we long for things to stay the same. Is this resistance a part of spiritual growth?*

JN: To be deprived of your habits makes you realize that you *are* your habits. From time to time something new arises within us that is not a habit, that is truly ourselves, but it's very fragile and likely to be overwhelmed by the repetitive functions we have identified with. The direction of true spiritual discipline is to pursue that fragile something-which-is-not-habit, and make it stronger. That's the real "I," the real Self, which is ordinarily the victim of our habits.

So a spiritual practice must confront our habits?

JN: Yes. You have to see habits for what they are, and not let their strength fool you. But that doesn't mean destroying them. They need to submit — habits are parts of ourselves intended to serve something higher and more authentic. As that authenticity becomes stronger within you, habits are less of an obstacle.

That sounds like an echo of the Christian idea that we must surrender our sinful, flawed nature. But to think of habit as sin seems moralistic and discouraging. Did this idea get off the track somewhere?

JN: Yes, it is just a little bit off; but that little bit is a lot, like leaping a chasm and missing the other cliff by just an inch. The moralistic tendency is to try to destroy our habits because we see them as evil. But evil is not inherent to our habits; evil arises when our habits are not related to our true self. Or, you could say that the real evil is a lack of relationship between the spiritual and the material parts of ourselves, the animal and the divine. They need to be related. When they're split, habit becomes all-powerful and we forget the self. The hatred of the body and condemnation of the material is part of what we call Puritanism. It's a great misunderstanding of the spiritual challenge.

It also seems that Westerners have a hard time understanding the notion of surrender. Either we keep our distance from it, or we latch onto it and want to surrender everything, and do whatever the guru says. What are the philosophical roots of our problem with surrender?

JN: It has to do with individualism, the scientific revolution, the Renaissance. . . We began to think for ourselves, to build and create, to do, and this became the Western genius of action. But eventually this autonomy blinded us to something higher in ourselves, the real source of our action. Simply put, we forgot God. This leads to great tension and uncertainty, as we lose our trust in the forces of life and nature. Then we must have control in order to prevent what might happen if we don't get our way. Doing and controlling get mixed up within us at a very deep level, and the fear of letting anything else take over gets repressive and deadening.

After we've had too much of that, of course, it can become sheer happiness to let it all go. Then we're all too willing to believe in anyone and anything. We surrender too easily because we've held on too tightly. With a little less investment in control, we'll have less naïveté in surrender.

In the East, the problem has centered on the ego as a false "I." In the West, it's expressed as a lack of contact with the unconscious. I think all people have difficulty with true surrender. Arjuna in the Bhagavad-Gita is very sad when he is told that he must fight and kill his relatives. That's a symbolic directive from Krishna to give up the dominance of certain parts of the personality. Christ gives a similar warning in the Bible, that you cannot love your mother or father before God. But if you seek the Kingdom of Heaven first, then all else is given to you. The first commandment is to love God; then follow all the social commandments. With the love of God first, all things fall into place.

Part of our problem with surrender has to do with spiritual romanticism, the aura that's conjured up when someone appeals to our fantasies with incense, robes, and spiritual language — all of which actually flatters us. When I ask my classes how Christ might appear to us today, most people still imagine a fellow in a robe.

What do you think of the contemporary "spiritual supermarket"? You seem to have sampled from many teachings.

JN: I think it's good to sample. The question is how much you want to buy. Somebody said that the sign of an authentic spiritual path is that it's difficult to get into and easy to get out of. So I'd think twice about those paths that look easy to get into, but difficult to leave.

The Secrets of Time and Love

How much of the deprivation felt by modern Westerners can be summed up by the complaints "If only I had more time..." and "If only I felt more love..."? (Throw in "more money" and you've just about got all our habitual wants summed up.) If Jacob Needleman is right, we will not find more love in the personal want ads, nor any extra time in a new smartphone app. Instead, we must turn these searches in on themselves to ask why we seek so incessantly for more of such immeasurables. By confronting our habitual desires and complaints, he suggests, we may pry open the door to the realm of the inner life — where both time and love reveal themselves not as problems to be solved but questions to be lived with.

"Such great questions cannot be answered with the part of the mind that solves problems," writes Needleman. "They need to be deeply felt and experienced long, long before they can begin to be answered." Yet it is in the very willingness to deeply feel and long experience the questions of time and love that we can begin to experience "enough" of both.

The following discussion was sparked by two of Needleman's books published early in the new millennium: THE WISDOM

OF LOVE (originally published as A LITTLE BOOK ON LOVE) and TIME AND THE SOUL. Because I happened to read these two volumes around the same time, I became intrigued by the interplay of the ideas in each, and proposed that we sit down to discuss them together. This conversation was originally published on the Fearless Books website.

We tend to think that both time and love are elusive or actively evading us. Your books suggest that we really don't need to search for either time or love, that what's more productive is to examine the search itself.

JN: Our relationship to time and love is conditioned by our state of being — our capacity to simply occupy our life, to be in touch with our real selves. The degree to which we're not in touch with the real self is the degree to which we are frustrated and driven crazy by lack of time, or find ourselves turning round and round either searching for or avoiding love in a way that's bitter and possibly degrading. The degree to which we are able to open to real presence — the "I am" or God within — is the degree to which we begin to have a human relationship to time and love.

It's that inner relationship that provides us with a center of gravity, the basis of meaning for everything else. When you feel a search or hunger for that inner presence, then you have some basis for a truly human relationship between two people that doesn't exist otherwise. To be supporting each other's inward search is a basis for love that has not been widely written about or understood.

You speak of sustained love as "a mystery in broad daylight." The most obvious meaning of "sustained" is "over time." How is the mystery of love sustained over time different from the mystery of falling in love?

JN: When you fall in love, it happens all by itself. It's not something you do deliberately, it more or less happens to you. There's no resistance from aspects of yourself that want to go another way; you're not struggling or trying to exercise your will or intention. There's no reckoning of time, and you're not aware of anything but the movement of falling in love.

We all know from such experiences of passion that while we are with the person we love, time stands still as if it doesn't exist. The sense of time that we're used to involves the mind and thinking, and is at the service of fear, planning, and manipulation. Those aspects of the self are what ordinarily make time into an enemy, and make us feel driven. Time re-enters the experience of falling in love only when fear comes back, when we begin to feel that we must hold onto the love, and don't want to let go. Or we start worrying about how this new love will fit into the rest of our lives. Then time seems to exert pressure again. But in the midst of the bliss of love, the mind and its fears has no authority at all.

Sustained love has to do with struggle. The automatic gift of love that is given to us by nature begins to change by encountering resistance — where something comes in against it, which is inevitable. When resistance appears, intention is required. People who can't make it past that point will go looking for another hit of automatic love; they'll want to fall in love over and over again because it doesn't require so much work. Because there always comes a point in the real love relationship when work is required, and that means working against all the impulses and distractions that we are heir to: other attractions, jealousy, sense of inadequacy, fear of responsibility, not to mention dealing with the simple day-to-day matters of life that can wear us down. These difficulties don't appear all at once; they occur over time, and that's why you must renew your intention many times to create sustained love.

You've written that "the Self is everything that the ego pretends to be, and the Self has the time that the ego searches for in vain." Is it only the Self that is capable of sustained love, and can the ego only "fall" in love?

JN: No, I think there's something in between the ego and the Self. Perhaps we could call it the noble part of the ego, that knows it has an unaccountable feeling in search of the Self. You might also call it the emerging soul. If the ego were completely insensitive, we wouldn't have a chance because the ego rules us mostly. But in most of us, the ego at least has a hint that there's something like the Self. That part of the ego struggles, and can have intentional love. The real Self doesn't struggle, because its very essence is love and compassion. When that appears there is no struggle.

In the Buddhist mahayana tradition, compassion appears all by itself when the ego is overcome. You don't have to develop it; it's part of human nature. In between the worst parts of the ego and the glory of the Self, there is this intermediate principle that is searching for completion.

Would you say then that we start falling out of love when the ego begins looking at its watch?

JN: Absolutely. Every woman knows that when a man starts looking at his watch... There's a saying in France that "love can withstand everything but a busy man." There are a lot of forces that can weigh against love, but basically time is the sum of all these forces; it enters into everything.

In your book about love you introduce an understanding of the philosophical stance known as Stoicism that differs from the popular notion that someone who is stoic is simply unfeeling or not admitting their suffering. How is real Stoicism related to love?

JN: The basic idea of Stoicism is that we are essentially one with the great self, or Logos of the universe. That's our true nature. We exercise that true nature by the capacity of the mind to relate consciously to its experiences — to accept, understand, or receive them without the preferences of liking or disliking those experiences, or responding with fear or craving. Nor does a true stoic try to reinterpret experiences, make them more or less dramatic, or good or bad. The stoic receives all experiences with an inner quiet.

This brings about a great inner freedom — the freedom of the person who is not devoured by emotional reactions. That doesn't mean he doesn't have these reactions; it means they don't toss him around. It's very wrong to think of a stoic as not caring. In fact the true stoic can act in a truly caring way because he's less at the service of his own egoistic emotions.

We tend to think that if we are in love we should be devoured by emotion, or at the very least, agitated to a high degree.

Doesn't passion mean that you can't live without the other person? We want that total captivity. We may feel insecure if we don't love that way, or don't feel loved that way. But a stoic doesn't love that way.

Perhaps the best popular icon we have for the stoic is the character Spock from the original Star Trek series. Why is Spock the most lovable figure from that show, the one who still touches fans the most? The idea about him was that he had no emotion, but in fact he had very strong feelings of loyalty, love, and justice. Captain Kirk was heroic too, but full of bombast and agitated emotions. And the other characters showed all kinds of neurosis. But Spock seemed to operate at a higher level, truly living by what he felt and believed without making a big show of his feelings. That's what made him a lasting and beloved icon.

It's also interesting to remember that Spock was the bastion of integrity — incapable of lying or manipulating to achieve his aims, as Captain Kirk often did.

JN: That's right. The stoic literally lives for truth; he feels truth, love, and loyalty to the core but is not swayed by his own self-interest. This points up the difference between what might one call "real feeling" and egoistic emotion. We are so used to egoistic emotions that we've often forgotten what real feeling is like.

In our culture there's often a conflict between the openness of women's feelings and the secrecy of men about their feelings, a stance which is often mistaken for stoicism. But true stoicism is not the same as keeping your feelings a secret.

JN: Completely different. A stoic may not give way to expressing certain emotions, which can make the rest of us nervous sometimes. But that is because he or she sees the usefulness — or lack thereof — of expressing a particular emotion in a given situation. At a high level of development, a stoic person can feel even a very strong passion or dislike, but govern its expression to benefit other people and the situation at hand.

When we refer to things as having a "timeless" quality, we really mean that their value will last for a very long time — not that they actually express the condition of no-time. Is it possible to say what timelessness is without referring to time?

JN: Within an experience of timelessness, the ego-driven mind is awe-struck and may even experience a great joy. It's that part of us that calls such an experience "timeless." But a timeless consciousness itself doesn't relate to time at all. In the section of my book on time called "The Arrival," a presence appears that is timeless — and the ego, always afraid of death, realizes that this presence is what it yearns to be. When a timeless presence attracts the ego, the ego is calmed; it is no longer a frightened animal.

Also in the time book, you write about a novel you are planning, in which a young man meets himself as an older man. Were you using this as a metaphor for the ego's meeting with the Self, that timeless presence? Do we approach maturity as we gain the capacity to see our inward future — that is, not what we'll be actually doing decades from now, but who we will have become in essence?

JN: Yes, and the reverse is also part of maturity. In my story the young man is inside the older one, as there is a younger presence within all of us. As we grow we have a tendency to cover over that eternal youth, but we have to get exposed to it again, see it again to know who we are. The seer — that older part of ourselves — has to develop a certain intensity and balance to confront this younger person, and deal with the shock of what that person is, with all of his immaturity, poor judgment, and so on.

You tell a wonderful legend about a young traveler crossing a desert who delays his own destiny to save a dying man who then tells him, "The desert will reward you." Late in his life, the traveler finds himself dying in the desert — and is rescued by his younger self. The message of this legend seems to be that we need to find ways to take care of the person we're becoming, not just the person we think we are now.

JN: Hope really lies in taking care of our own inner possibilities. If you don't take care of that, you'll end up on the porch of the old folks' home feeling bitter. We're mortal, we're going to die, life is short — and because of all that, we can't look for all of our meaning in what we're doing right now. There is something beyond our mortality and our circumstances in the finite world that we're meant to take care of. If there is not that timeless thing within us, then it's a stupid universe after all!

Yet when we look for love — as in the personals — we look for people who will suit our preferences, wishes, and circumstances in the material world. And some people get very specific! Can you imagine what someone looking for "sustained love" would write in a personal ad? Or would one simply not advertise?

JN: Perhaps one wouldn't advertise. But if so, one might say that he or she is looking for a love that's not devouring, that supports the search for truth in each other, and that doesn't take each other's delusions too seriously.

You've written that "when we actually feel another's struggle for inner freedom, we cannot help but love." Why?

JN: I don't know why. It's just an empirical fact to me. When I see someone struggling for the Self, it touches the same search and struggle within myself. It's a relatively rare kind of love, but not so rare. If you've ever witnessed someone struggling to become more honest and sincere, or to overcome some weakness, then you know what this kind of love is.

When I was travelling overseas once and found myself without money or food — and not looking very reputable — I came upon a woman in her garden and asked her for food. She said, "Are you really that hungry?" I said yes, and I watched all kinds of feelings show in her face for a few moments, from fear to compassion. I could see her struggling, and she finally looked at me and said, "I have nothing." Yet somehow I felt great warmth for her at that moment. Even as she turned me down, I could see her struggling toward her Self.

That reminds me of something else you wrote about love: "We seem to expect of the other what we ourselves could not give." Do we have a similar expectation of time — that is, we think we need more time to find a sense of freedom that we may already be avoiding?

JN: It's a good point; I hadn't thought of that. The passage of time itself will not give us what comes only from a certain inner awareness, and in fact we may use time to avoid that awareness. Time gives wisdom only if there's a corresponding inward activity, an engagement with the processes of self-confrontation and growth. And time heals, if we let it. Even the most fervent resentments tend to fade over time, more quickly if we help them along. Whether we're speaking of time or a lover, we always need to question whether we're asking of the other what we need to give.

You've written that we're actually "built for the happiness that comes from the cultivation of a deeper power of mind and feeling than is offered to us by the automatic process of emotions." Isn't that deeper kind of happiness pretty rare?

JN: Anyone who's working on themselves, searching for themselves in an intelligent way, touches this feeling of happiness more and more often, if only for a moment at a time. So I don't think it's all that rare. It's just that the culture we're in doesn't know how to help us appreciate such experiences. In fact life itself gives us this kind of happiness at unexpected moments. For instance, in a time of great loss, you may be suddenly touched by a certain strange kind of joy because you've lost the thing you wanted, but then discovered another kind of freedom that you would never know if you always got what you wanted.

And what happens to one's sense of time in these moments?

JN: There's no fear anymore. Obsession with time always has to do with fear, and so in these moments of touching a greater freedom we realize that time is not the enemy. We escape the concept of linear time and enter cyclical time, in which we realize that time is continually renewing and giving back to us, not just taking away our youth or energy in the way that linear time seems to do.

Why do you think the metaphor of "just in time" is so compelling? In action and suspense movies, for instance, the bomb is defused or the code is broken with only seconds to spare — never a couple minutes or an hour. Why do we have such a strong sense of a countdown, that we're only going to avoid catastrophe at the last second? From the philosophical viewpoint, what happens when "time runs out"?

JN: Off the top of my head I would say that our fear of time running out is a way of expressing the strength of evil. We have a sense that evil is equal to good — Moriarty was always as smart as Holmes — and this results in a major battle within us between these equal and opposed forces. What happens "just in time" is the influx of miraculous, reconciling spiritual energy from above and beyond our inner battlefield.

Of course it's not really good and evil in traditional religious terms that are fighting each other; it's our seeking for the Self and our own resistance to that seeking. Left to our own devices, we'd never resolve the battle. It's the miracle of spirit coming from out of nowhere that resolves the inner struggle. When the action hero suddenly knows what to do, has an intuitive flash about breaking the code or snipping the right wire on the bomb, that could be taken as a metaphor for the arrival of spiritual insight. Something comes from another level — just as the hero is about to give up on saving himself or the world, the magic of spirit appears. This is what we know will save us in the nick of time.

The Meanings of Money

In his book MONEY AND THE MEANING OF LIFE, Jacob Needleman tells a story that illustrates just how difficult it can be to deal with money honestly and straightforwardly — a difficulty that may only be exacerbated by having a "spiritual" outlook. In October 1967, just after San Francisco's famed Summer of Love, the young professor entered a shop on Haight Street that offered a number of exotic religious icons for sale: "Jewish prayer shawls, Tibetan bells and vajras and countless other objects that I had never seen anywhere except in the solemn environment of churches or temples."

Drawn to a prayer shawl priced at $35, Needleman pulled out his checkbook only to be told by the flower-child clerk that the store accepted nothing but cash. Offended, Needleman assured her that he was good for the money and added, "Do you know who I am? I'm Jacob Needleman! I'm a professor at San Francisco State University!"

As I am spitting out this absurdity, my eyes fall upon the photograph that happens to be on the wall just behind her. Having just heard my mouth express the most pompously egotistical sounds I had ever consciously heard it utter, I now find myself being observed by Gautama Buddha himself, whose teaching about the illusion of ego I had just that morning so carefully explained to my students at the university.

The comedy continues. "Let me speak to the owner!" I demand. The salesgirl disappears and returns accompanied by a man in his late twenties with unkempt hair, soft, watery eyes, a sickeningly loving smile, and a small photograph of a Hindu, presumably his guru, hanging around his neck. I repeat my demands, adding something to the effect — thank God, I don't remember my exact words — that not only am I a professor, but a professor of philosophy and religion and give courses in the very people whose photographs are on the wall. As though that in itself entitled me to pay by check.

Suddenly, the man with the sickening smile develops eyes hard as steel and somehow, without his altering the smallest muscle in his lips, the "loving" smile is transformed into a sardonic grin. He picks up the prayer shawl — for a fleeting moment I actually imagine he is going to offer it to me as a gift — and while he is reverently folding it, he advises me to perform a sexual act upon myself.

Back in the street, a team of Hare Krishnas in full regalia and painted faces march by, chanting their Hindu mantra. I am trembling with anger — but at what or whom? And as one of the Hare Krishnas asks me to buy some incense or something, I suddenly burst into laughter. But, again, at what or at whom?

As this story suggests, it can seem that money has the power to make us act in ways that are contrary to our avowed beliefs and values. But is it really money that evokes these negative transformations in our character? Or is it, rather, that money somehow peels away our hypocrisies and reveals us as we really are?

For it should also be said that money can be the medium of great good deeds, besides providing the lifeblood of all the commerce that makes civilization possible. Money has become such an indispensable, unavoidable centerpiece of our daily lives that we tend to regard it as an incontrovertible force of nature — when, in fact, it is no more or less than what we make of it. We get so obsessed with "making money," and so worried about how our governments, banks, and investment firms are handling our funds, that we forget it's a completely human invention that depends on our belief and faith in it to have any power at all. In the long run, we may have more to gain from deeply examining all the meanings of money than from trying to devise yet another strategy for managing it.

Money and what we do with it are not usually in the purview of philosophy.

JN: Yes, and that connects to all that I'm doing in philosophy: trying to relate the great spiritual ideas about life, God, and the universe, especially the perennial questions of the heart, to the nitty-gritty problems of our everyday life in this world. My whole work has been looking for that bridge between the philosophical and the everyday. Until I wrote my book on money, hardly anyone had written about its spiritual meaning — i.e., what it means in the life of someone who has a goal or focus of spiritual development. Some spiritual teachers were writing on the subject, but they were usually too idealistic, suggesting that we should be "free of money" and so forth. One of my mentors had suggested, "If you want to see the measure of a human being, see how he or she deals with money, sex, and time." That was the origin of MONEY AND THE MEANING OF LIFE.

It's actually impossible to be "free of money," isn't it?

JN: Yes, impossible. And often the very same spiritual teachers who would urge you to be inwardly free of monetary concerns — like they are, presumably — will be hitting you up to buy their book or make a donation to their teaching, almost in the same breath. The first thing you see when you try to penetrate the hypocrisy around money is that this social technology called money enters into every corner and pocket of human life. You cannot escape the money question; it follows you wherever you go. Everything now is enveloped in commoditization or monetization. Things that you would never have dreamt could be monetized — like the value of a life in a wrongful death lawsuit, or the value of a housewife's years of work at home, in a divorce settlement — are now quantified in dollars. Money enters into everything we do, but hardly anyone faces what it really means.

Was there a time when money wasn't so pervasive?

JN: Yes, there was, but that doesn't mean human beings were free of that part of themselves that is taken by money. But it took different forms. Nowadays, money has taken the place of so many other kinds of valuation in human life.

When I was a child, we had a family doctor who came and visited us. Sometimes we gave him a five or ten dollar bill, sometimes we offered him a meal. Of course he needed money and we paid him in some form, but the relationship between our family and the doctor came first. I remember the shock I felt when we got our first bill in the mail from a doctor, saying "this is what you owe." Now that seems obvious and normal; back then it was not normal to get a bill. I remember thinking, "So medicine is a business. I thought it was a calling!" Of course you'd pay people who followed their callings, and sometimes people who followed the medical calling got rich, but still, I grew up in a time when you didn't look on medicine as a way to make money. That has changed radically. The calling hasn't gone away, of course, but it's now much more contaminated with money at every level.

Isn't there a connection between the monetization of medicine and its increasing technology?

JN: Of course, because our growing scientific technology demands money. But the human dimension of medicine is definitely in danger. The conversion of medicine to a business has taken away so much of human contact, which is really necessary for good medical care. In a very real way, money has replaced relationship in medical practice, making it less personal, and also taking away a lot of the satisfaction of being a doctor. Some physicians have even started leaving the practice simply because they can't keep up with the paperwork; not medical records per se, but the incredible workload now required by the business side of medicine. Doctors spend so little time now with patients, in the same room. The work of listening to a patient is a key part of medical diagnosis and treatment. Without that, the help and the curing that medicine is intended to provide are greatly reduced.

To get a diagnosis, a doctor used to stay with patients, listening, intuiting, even smelling them, to take the time to understand what was going on. Not only did that help with diagnosis, the "staying with" the patient actually helped with healing.

I've always felt uneasy about the way that spirituality gets monetized. In spiritual circles, for instance, it's not uncommon to see the request for a "love offering" replacing a simple price. It's as if spiritual teachers or organizations don't want to call out money by name, perhaps because they feel guilty about putting a price tag on spiritual wisdom or experience.

JN: Part of the challenge here is to understand what aspect of human life money is necessary for. What part of the whole human being is involved with money? An essential part of our nature is indeed expressed and organized by money. But we are two-natured beings. A part of ourselves is meant to function out in the world and interact with material things, and a part of ourselves is meant to search for ultimate truth for its own sake, trying to open inwardly to something higher within ourselves, something beyond everyday experience in the material world.

Those two parts of ourselves are definitely dissonant, and we are here to find the balance between them, to develop the capacity to embrace both parts and let each play its proper role in a whole human life.

But I don't think that balance is struck simply by renaming a price as a love offering.

JN: I should say not! Rather, that's a symptom of unease about reconciling the disparate parts of ourselves. Part of the answer is not to force the material and the spiritual together. When you're doing business, you just do business. When you pray, you just pray. But don't get the two mixed up.

People often entertain a spiritual fantasy about money, that gets expressed in the idea that "God will provide" by sending them money when they need it. In New Age terms, it gets expressed in ideas like the Law of Attraction, but it's magical thinking either way. Ninety-eight percent of the time, it's just fantasy.

And yet, there is a kernel of truth in these ideas that contributes to their perennial popularity. It is true that when you really have a deep, energetic wish that corresponds to something very needed, strange things can begin to happen with money. Sometimes, just when you're down and out and seem to have no further resources or any chance of finding any, there's suddenly a check in the mail that you didn't expect. You could easily call it chance, but somehow you know it isn't.

What do we not understand about money?

JN: In our culture, one of the great potentials of money is that it can help you see yourself as you really are — that is, it can provoke a confrontation with hypocrisy that leads you to see what you're really doing and what you actually believe. For most people, that's going to be a profound shock.

Let's say your best friend asks you to spot him a hundred

bucks. For some, that's easy; for others, it can mean an uneasy moment of assessing what they really feel about a friend. Or let's say that you have a great plan for a business that your friends are all enthusiastic about... until you ask for some investment money. In such moments, things become very real and concrete. You find out what you really believe in, as opposed to mere ideals that you like to say you believe in.

That's a good thing about money, in a spiritual sense. Money can serve many kinds of functions. It can also be an instrument of love, a genuine gift.

There's some historical evidence that money was an invention meant to help people share things and experience communion — like sharing bread. As communities became bigger and more complicated and simple barter became impractical, money became a representation of something meant to be shared. The first real coins that were made were imprinted with gods or other divine symbols on one side and some kind of material symbol on the other side, like a castle or other important building. So money was originally meant to be a symbol of both spirit and materiality, to help us manage our lives and our interrelationships. It was not meant to divide us into classes or warring factions; it was meant to be unitive. Gradually, of course, as things both decayed and developed, money became what it is now, a much more complicated central fact of our lives.

I don't think we can understand the problems of money until we understand human nature. Money is what it is because of what we are; how could anyone dispute that?

But I think most people respond to money as if it's a force of nature that's beyond our control. It seems to be imposed upon us, as part of a divine or natural order, yet it's a total fiction we've created.

JN: Yes, but what isn't? Imagine that you're at a party talking to a stranger who's pretty dull, and you do everything you can to get away from him. Then someone else whispers to you that the stranger is quite wealthy. Does he suddenly become more interesting? Are you tempted to think that if you get close to him, become his friend, somehow some of his money will "rub off" on you or become yours? How much of money is a fantasy in this way, an imaginary or magical force?

Well, I've always thought that a lottery represents a dispensation of grace. It's as if God will come down from heaven and just give us this magic stuff that eases all our problems. God is the dispenser of luck, in a sense. To me that's the compulsion of gambling, or that desire to sidle over and be friends with the wealthy person — it's a substitute for the grace of God.

JN: Paper money itself is a fantasy, or representation of magic in that way. It's not "real" in the way that a cow that you could get milk from, or barter with, is real. And it's not even the same as gold, which to many people seems more real despite its intrinsic uselessness. Gold is only so valuable because everybody wants it. Why does everybody want it? Because it's valuable! People are constantly searching for some way to establish value, and they choose something and just assign great value to it — hence the "gold standard" that some people believe we should return to, in lieu of all this paper money with no real "value" behind it.

It's as if the gold standard becomes the last article of faith when the religion of money is otherwise failing us. We arbitrarily decide that gold is incorruptible; it simply cannot lose its value, as if by fiat.

JN: When enough people believe such a fiction, it's no longer a fiction. And obviously, many people live out their whole lives believing in many such "realities." Even Henry Ford, the iconic American capitalist, once said that if people were told what was really backing up their money, there would be riots in the streets the next day. In fact we've seen that happen across many cultures, including ours, when money suddenly seems to lose its value — which is to say that we no longer trust in it, in the way that we usually do. There's a very real sense in which we can look at our whole creation of money as a fake system, a kind of Ponzi scheme. It only works while you have faith in it; besides that faith, there's nothing real about it.

And on a day to day basis, the condition of the economy seems to have less to do with real circumstances than with whatever we believe is going on. Wall Street goes up and down depending on the emotional insecurity of brokers and investors at any given time, rather than real data-driven changes in the market.

JN: It all rides on promises and beliefs, depending on how much we feel we can trust the fantasy of money from moment to moment. Money certainly seems very real when you put it down on the table to buy something, but if you take a closer look at what that money actually represents and how its value is determined... no, it's just not real. But if money is fake, then what is there about our lives that is real?

This is a crucial spiritual question. The economist Max

Weber showed that capitalism is fueled by religious fervor, the Calvinistic belief that amassing wealth proves you are one of God's elect. And I think just about everyone does revere wealth, even those who say they don't care about it. From time to time there arise movements to live communally in a spirit of equality and shared resources, shunning individual wealth, and ninety percent of those movements fail within one generation. Why? Because they don't honestly take into account human nature, which includes desire, greed, egoism, and a drive for individual power.

We certainly don't live in a culture in which you're shunned if you start making more money than you need for yourself or your family! That attitude simply wouldn't even occur to us; "making more" is always a good thing. Yet the spiritual message of many traditions is that as a "child of God" we really need nothing but grace, or salvation, or enlightenment. It just seems impossible to actually live by that attitude on a daily basis.

JN: Yes, because you do need food, shelter, and safety for you and your family. You need to deal with threats on all sides, from other people and from nature itself. You need to invent, adapt, and develop as a human being, otherwise you simply can't function. To an extent not really seen before in our history, all these necessities of being now require money as a means of practical exchange.

Now we do have the capacity for what Lewis Hyde called "the gift" — the capacity to give with no expectation for return or reward, and no hidden egoism. While altruism often turns out to be good for the giver, there does exist genuine altruism without a self-serving motive. The moment that we do start calculating the possible returns on a gift, then it loses the entire quality of a gift, and just becomes a form of exchange again — and quite likely a dishonest exchange, because now we are pretending to give while awaiting a return on our investment.

When you really give, you are free of the mentality that normally drives us, and that drives most of culture for that matter. You come into contact with a deeper aspect of your being than you would know otherwise: a part that's not subject to hypocrisy, social convention, or religious propriety. It's the part of us that's "real" in a way that money is not, and I think that there's a fundamental human drive just to be real... maybe even more fundamental than the drive to survive, succeed, or get rich.

Money can make you feel valued or important, but the significance that it imparts is a fantasy. It's temporary, and it can go away if you lose your money. The realness that comes with true giving is not a fantasy, and it has a timeless quality.

That reminds me of the story from your book about the young wealthy man who was studying the subject of money in a small class of yours, and who once tried to give you a gold bar, out of an almost desperate need to be recognized and valued.

JN: Yes, that kind of giving is often pathological, driven by a compulsive need that will never be satisfied by getting or giving money away. There is a sad tendency for some über-wealthy people to be terribly lonely and even self-loathing, because they know that most people around them are literally "there for the money." I know some people would say, "Oh, I could handle that kind of self-loathing; just give me enough money." And to that

I'd say, "Like hell you could."

You don't have to repay a real gift; as someone once told me, the only way to repay a true gift is to accept it. I've sometimes asked my students whether they've ever done something for someone without anyone knowing that it was done — and which cost them something in order to do it. Very few people could answer that. One woman who did said that it evoked an entirely new feeling for her, something she'd never experienced before. And I suspect that what was awakened in her was the knowledge that we are born to serve. It's a fundamental part of our nature that has been covered over with so many layers of hypocrisy and cynicism that we've mostly lost touch with it. We confuse it with volunteerism and charity and other moralistic forms of being "good," but it's none of those attitudes.

Is it hopeless to fix money?

JN: That's like asking if it's hopeless to fix humankind. We can make this or that correction to the economy or to banking or the stock market to fix certain problems, but the whole problem of money will never be solved as long as humanity is egoistic. So we have to find a way to deal with money that minimizes the negative effects of egoism on society as a whole. Regulations and laws and law enforcement can induce temporary improvements, but for a bigger change we have to have a moral ideal for money that penetrates society. By "moral ideal" I mean an ideal that appeals to people's better nature, in some way that neither capitalism, nor socialism, nor communism has ever managed to do.

That's interesting to me, because despite my own sympathies for the recent "Occupy" protests that occurred around the nation, it seems like an inherently anarchic movement without either an agenda or a coherent philosophy. Unlike the Tea Party, which unfortunately got a number of activists elected to positions of power, the Occupiers don't seem to have a clear moral idea around which to organize. They know that the current system is flawed, but there's no solution being proposed. They are able to say only that "greed is wrong" and seem to think that if we protest loudly enough against greed, it will somehow go away.

JN: This kind of movement can induce forms of temporary change, like moving some furniture around when you need to tear down the house and build a new one. But that's not to say that temporary changes are useless. They can buy us enough time to keep searching inwardly for the real changes we need. Every society has some degree of corruption; the salient question for every society is, "How much corruption can we bear?"

No society is ever going to be pure, but part of what we are looking at now is whether our degree of corruption has gone past a bearable limit. For many people in the United States, it has gone past that, and part of what Occupy seems to be saying is "This is all wrong!" So there is, perhaps, an instinctive recognition that we need to get back to the deeper reality within ourselves… and for that, there is no political solution. You can't elect anybody on that platform.

The point is that you can't change society until people change, from the inside out. That's a spiritual process that can't be legislated or regulated. But you can make some rational, systemic changes in society that allow our spiritual progress to proceed, instead of discouraging it. If we become, as a society, a little less enamored of greed, then we have a better chance of confronting greed deep within ourselves, where the problem really is.

So money is not the root of all evil, after all.

JN: No, but the love of money can be — or more precisely, the love of all the illusions we have about money. Money can serve any obsession we have, and many of our obsessions are served or exaggerated by money these days. But seen properly, money is the primary means we have for organizing one half of human nature — the earthly half, the outer self that does things in the world — as opposed to the inner self. Money is a very important social technology that can serve our best earthly purposes. And how well we use that technology says a lot about how we are managing our inner and outer selves, how well they are communicating with each other. Our culture's problems with money reflect the fact that our outer lives tend to be getting more and more disconnected from our deeper, inner life. So when money itself seems to be evil, it's really only an effect of the rupture of human nature — the disconnection between inner, higher values and our everyday life in the world.

There was a distinct philosophical split in the 2012 Presidential campaign, in which one side maintained that the accumulation of wealth is the engine of prosperity — and therefore we shouldn't overtax the wealthy — and the other side essentially maintained that there's a limit to any societal good that private wealth provides, and therefore we should tax the wealthy more. Do you feel there's any inherent virtue or vice in wealth?

JN: Some people are born into wealth, and they are also bred with a certain ethic that leads them to do good with their money. The ethic of using wealth to help others does exist. But there are certainly those who use wealth as a self-indulgence, or for power tripping. It's well known that winning the lottery ruins many of the winners' lives. So what wealth does is amplify the tendencies that already exist within us. If you are a mean-spirited, poor son of a bitch, then if you come into a lot of money you will likely become a mean-spirited, wealthy son of a bitch.

People strive for wealth partly because of the idea that it will make them safe. And it does make them safe from certain things, at least temporarily — from poverty, from the circumstances of cold and hunger, and so forth. But you're going to have emotional difficulties regardless, and wealth can introduce a whole new set of difficulties. Those include the fallacious idea that you're somehow better than others, or above them; it also includes anxieties about losing your wealth. You may be pressured by flattery and other social strategies intended, ultimately, to separate you from some of your wealth. If you don't know how to deal with all that, then wealth can ultimately make you less safe than you were before.

What inner quality has to be present in people if wealth is not to corrupt them?

JN: The answer to that has to begin with the idea that the proper use of wealth is to serve, in some way, the inner growth of the individual. I think another necessary characteristic would be humility, which usually derives from confrontation with the realities of life, death, suffering, and sorrow — all those things that wealth doesn't protect you from. I've known many wealthy people who are deeply humble, and they all have the interest of wanting to use their wealth to help others. And they are realistic people, in the sense of having confronted some serious difficulties of life head-on, without their wealth making much difference in those confrontations.

All this touches on an even deeper question, that is: What is a good person? A good person does good things, which sounds rather obvious. But doing good things doesn't come from being religiously correct, or following the rules, or happening to be good by accident. Goodness comes from having a strong inner life.

At a certain level, even a level that we might call middle-class, wealth comes with prison bars because it enslaves us to our society. You might own a nice house on a beautiful street — but that means you have to worry about how it looks, and whether you can keep up with the mortgage, what precautions you have to take against being burglarized, and so on. You're not really free to just walk away, in most cases.

There's also the naïve belief that all wealth should simply be given away, redistributed, and that if we did so, all the world's problems would be solved.

JN: There are certainly people who have given away everything they had, and they have thrived, but they are relatively few. I think it's more important to have an intelligent sense of honor that enables you to use your wealth, however great or little it is, in a way that helps yourself and others. We do have an obligation to ourselves that is the very opposite of selfishness — and it is ultimately an obligation to realize the inner potentials we are born with. You might have the potential to work in the Peace Corps for no money and do great good there, or you might have the potential to become the CEO of a large corporation for a great deal of money, yet do just as much good there. Whether you're capable of selfless love and intelligent "right action" is not determined by how much money you have, or don't have.

Some years ago I was teaching philosophy in a business school where the students wanted to hone their managerial skills in the environment of a humanistic education. The questions that intrigued us were "What is a good human being?" and "What are the characteristics of a good businessperson?" We were looking for the overlap of those two questions, because the fact is that business in one form or another occupies about eighty percent of our lives. We have to buy things and sell things; we have to be in business or deal with some kind of business every day; we have to make a living when we work for others, or a profit when we work for ourselves. You can't run a business or make a good living if you just give away all your money. So giving, all by itself, doesn't define a good businessperson. Part of being in business or dealing with businesses means being tough, but not cruel; it also means being sensitive to human needs, but not soft or mushy. These questions and their answers are fascinating because a lot of what makes a good businessperson is the same as what makes a good human being. There's a balance of qualities that isn't so easily defined, when you really start thinking about it.

You've suggested that what we don't understand about money is that it's secondary — that is, it's not the most important thing in our lives, but it's usually the second most important thing. For too many people in America, money is the most important thing in their lives, even if they deny it. And when they deny it, people often err in the other direction and say money is just not important at all. So if money should be second in our priorities, what comes first?

JN: The spiritual study of money and the role it plays in our lives is very important. But money itself is not spiritual. What comes first is self-knowledge — and one of the best ways to get self-knowledge is to study our relationship to money, because money represents the material side of our lives. No matter how spiritual you think you are, you cannot deny that you have a material side, and you cannot live on this earth without being material. We don't deal with our material side by denying it, but by keeping it in its place — which is second place.

Searching for the Soul of America

SEVERAL months after the fall of the World Trade Center in September 2001, President George W. Bush held a press conference at which he was asked by a reporter how the immense tragedy had changed him personally. The Chief Executive hesitated briefly before answering, "Ask my wife.... I don't spend much time looking in the mirror."

In his response, Bush revealed much about the contemporary American character: We are a people of action who don't spend much time reflecting on our actions, our motives, or ourselves. We simply presume that we're good folks who have everyone's best interest at heart — and then proceed to persuade, cajole, and intimidate the rest of the world's peoples to accept our well-intentioned actions, whether they like them or not.

But when those immense towers crashed to earth with such a stunning loss of life, our still-young nation's forward momentum seemed to come to a halt. Suddenly we realized that we would "never be the same" and that the time might have come to start taking stock of our lives in a new way. Even Larry King said so.

If Jacob Needleman is right, America was always meant to be a place where deep reflection and assessment of one's values, motives, and potential could flourish. In his book THE AMERICAN SOUL: *Rediscovering the Wisdom of the Founders,* Needleman writes that "America was once the hope of the world," and not just because it symbolized political liberty and freedom from want. "The deeper hope of America was its vision of what humanity is and can become." In the book he uses the writings and speeches of such icons as Washington, Franklin, Jefferson, and Lincoln to delineate his transformative vision of America.

But Needleman gives equal time in his book to what he calls "the crimes of America" — namely, our early legacy of slavery and the genocide of the Native American people. "To a great extent, the material success of America rests on these crimes and others like them," he says. But he urges his readers to take stock of America's virtues and failures in a way that might yield more telling sentiments than pride on the one hand or guilt on the other.

"The great wisdom," he writes, "whispers to us from ancient times of another kind of confrontation with what is good and what is evil in ourselves; another kind of hope, compared to which that which we call optimism is dangerously naïve and childish; and another kind of remorse, compared to which that which we call guilt is impotent and self-deceitful."

The self-confrontation Needleman suggests is the kind of inner work that eventually yields more than just a new opinion of ourselves. It is the work that slowly but surely yields a new self entirely. Perhaps by such a process America itself might eventually achieve the potential that our Founding Fathers glimpsed. But the process will be considerably more difficult than simply asking our spouses how we're doing.

In your book you argue that the Founding Fathers intentionally created a constitutional framework that would allow the inner life of the citizenry to flourish. How do you know whether they really meant for Americans to develop their inner lives?

JN: I can't say what actually went on in their minds, but when I look at their writings, I do see signs of the spiritual quest. The spirituality of this country does not necessarily have to do with sectarian religion. Spirituality simply means inwardness of the unselfish variety. It's very clear that the Founders' ideas of individuality had nothing to do with the adolescent concept of individuality that we have today — that is, doing or saying anything one wants in order to appear clever and original. To many of the Founders, individuality meant the effort to acknowledge and obey the higher law within.

For a government even to suggest that part of its function is to guarantee its citizens' right to "the pursuit of happiness" strikes me as an essentially mystical undertaking. Has any other nation put forth happiness as part of its vision?

JN: If you view happiness in terms of self-realization and spiritual fulfillment, then the great theocracies of ancient times, such as in India and Tibet, were essentially devoted to the happiness of their people. For Plato, and many others after him, the whole purpose of governance was to enable people to relate to "the Good" — his word for God, or "the highest reality." But of course it may be that no actual government has ever fulfilled that ideal.

We also have to recognize a distinction made by Thomas Paine, concerning the difference between government and society. He argued that government is necessarily tough and punitive and often operates by the sanction of physical force. Society, on the other hand, is softer, more aesthetic and ethical; it's the way humans relate to each other.

Nations are not people. They are a lower, not higher, organism that cannot be judged the way we judge individual human beings. Nations must have honorable values and not be fundamentally criminal, but a nation exists primarily to protect its society.

If you confuse these two concepts, you may believe that a government should behave like the society it defends. That's a serious mistake and can lead to misplaced criticism of the way government operates. In my book I suggest that the deepest purpose of the United States government is to provide conditions under which our society can flourish spiritually as well as materially. That doesn't mean that we should expect our government or its functionaries to be spiritual or to have a highly developed consciousness.

What exactly did the Founding Fathers mean by "happiness"?

JN: Obviously the happiness they were talking about has nothing to do with wish fulfillment or getting everything you want. In fact, every spiritual teaching will tell you that wish fulfillment definitely isn't happiness. The great discovery of adulthood is that getting what you want doesn't by itself make you happy.

What does make you happy is to establish contact with a principle within yourself that orders your life and opens you up to loving others, and to loving something higher than yourself.

So happiness is discovering truth within yourself, and then trying to live according to that truth. The Founders understood that this kind of happiness can be pursued only by a society with a certain type of government — one that would allow us the political liberty to search for conscience, while also allowing us the material support that this search requires. As a society, we do need material well-being, but our ultimate purpose is the search for conscience. I think that is what the Founding Fathers meant by "the pursuit of happiness." I'm calling for a new mythology, a new story of America. I believe that many of the Founders had an impulse and an intent to look within.

What's the difference between mythologizing the Founders and simple hero worship?

JN: To mythologize is to bring whatever a great person stood for into a concrete, emotionally valid focus — a useful representation of an ideal. Hero worship is childish or adolescent and often based on unimportant qualities. It says that a great man or woman was a better human being than everyone else. That's why hero worship is shattered by the discovery of the hero's weaknesses.

A person achieves mythological status when he or she represents an ideal greater than his or her personal character. For instance, Thomas Jefferson represents the ideal of equality espoused in the Declaration of Independence. The fact that he owned slaves may cause us to think less of him as a person, but it does not necessarily detract from his myth.

What we know of Jefferson suggests that he understood the crime of slavery precisely because he owned slaves. Regarding slavery, he once wrote, "When I consider that God is just, I fear for the future of our country." He knew that the country had the wolf by the ears; it couldn't let go of it, and it couldn't defeat it. Real passion for change is rooted in remorse. I think he personally felt the crime of slavery and knew that it had to change, whether he could manage that change in his own life or not. Very few people today would say they believe in polluting the environment, but most of us drive cars. Jefferson, too, participated in a sin of his times. But what he believed in, fought for, and accomplished transcends his personal sins and weaknesses.

For all their vision, didn't the Founding Fathers grant the rights and freedoms conferred by the Constitution to a fairly narrow population — that is, white men like themselves?

JN: My aim in this book was not to draw conclusions about whether the Founding Fathers lived up to their ideals, or whether their vision was incomplete because it applied, in their time, mostly to white males. My aim was to write a metaphysical poem about America and what it means, including its dark side.

Having said that, I think it was probably impossible to get our Constitution, as good as it is, ratified in the real world without there being some bad in it, too. Faced with the conflicting needs of the different colonies and an economy that depended in part on slavery, the Constitution's framers could never have brought the country together had they tried to impose the pure ideals suggested by the language they used. I believe that many of them did seek equality and justice for all, regardless of race and gender, but they knew those goals were not achievable in their time.

Indeed, we're still working toward those goals today. We've made some progress, but we've lost ground in other ways. Who knows whether an eighteenth-century person might look at the twenty-first century as morally degraded?

You say that "self-improvement" was at the heart of early American individualism. Is that the same as what we think of today as "self-help"?

JN: Self-help is certainly not the same thing as the self-improvement pursued by people like Washington and Franklin. For early Americans, self-improvement meant "movement toward virtue." It meant developing your character by your deliberate intention; it meant developing both will and good will. It meant having the ability to see the truth, not to indulge in slander or vengeance, and to care for others: in other words, being what my Yiddish-speaking grandmother used to call a *mensch* — a person of authentic virtue.

Self-improvement is not therapeutic; it does not mean feeling better about yourself. The two goals may not be opposed, but their overlap is slight. Self-respect is involved in self-improvement, as long as you understand that the self you respect is not the ego.

We seem to have no popular concept of a person who may be troubled, or living a difficult life, because he or she is "moving toward virtue."

JN: I don't think we even know about such people. Who are they? Where do you find them? They're still out there somewhere, I think.

Rather, we are steeped in the idea that our childhood traumas or our genes have essentially determined our lives.

JN: We have left out the notion of individual will. When I talk to my classes about what an ideal or highly developed human being might be like, they bring up virtues like compassion, wisdom, kindness, and so on. But nobody ever mentions will; it's almost as if the word has fallen out of our vocabulary. If I write the word *will* on the blackboard, my students have a hard time recognizing what I mean, but once they do, they become very interested in it.

Will is the means by which we overcome the problems that life or genes have handed us. Without it, there is no true character. Ironically, will may be what's missing in many people's attempts to feel better about themselves.

You say that Washington was known for his strength of will. What else should we remember about him?

JN: Washington was important for the way that he let go of power. Not only did he have great will, strength, and presence, but at his peak of influence following the Revolutionary War — when he could have seized the kind of power that most people would crave, when he could literally have become "king of America" — he retired as general of the Revolutionary Army and went home. That was in 1783. The first presidential election was not until 1792, so there was a long period in which he held no power. I don't see this decision as a political ploy, the way that we would tend to think of it today; I think he was genuinely interested in the good of the nation. His will and his ability to let go are Washington's trademarks for me.

Unfortunately, the prevalent myths we have about him involve cherry trees and bad teeth.

Likewise, all we usually recall about Benjamin Franklin is his kite-flying.

JN: Well, Franklin didn't just fly a kite. This man played with lightning, a great force of nature, at considerable risk to himself. And the discoveries he made were significant; the lightning rod was one practical result of what he did. He also deduced the nature of electricity, that it has positive and negative charges, which was a genuine scientific discovery.

You could say that Franklin was distinguished by the degree of risk he took in almost everything he did, from science to political revolution. At the same time, he was a terrifically effective foreign ambassador. Getting the French on our side in the Revolutionary War was a crucial political achievement.

Of the Founding Fathers, Franklin seems to have had the most "star power" in his day.

JN: In Europe, in any case. Washington was certainly as well-known there, but Franklin was a great socializer and knew how to mingle in the right circles of power. Overseas he was "the American" in a way that no one had yet managed to be, a human symbol of a new nation. Yet he also had a strong inner life, and he concentrated on self-improvement, in a moral and ethical fashion that we have hardly any grasp of today. He was bent on becoming more virtuous, an idea that sounds old-fashioned to us now.

In the 2000 presidential election, we saw the judicial system politically manipulated in a way that allowed the will of the people, as expressed in the popular vote, to be defeated. More recent scandals at the highest levels of business and finance are pointing up the immense danger of corporate power and corruption, a force the Founding Fathers did not foresee. Given all this, do you think we're living in an especially dangerous time for the American soul?

JN: No matter how beautifully conceived, no government by itself can make a country virtuous. You must also have the good will and morality of the people who serve the government, and of the nation's populace. The Founders recognized the inevitable danger of what they called the "passions" — lust, greed, violence, hatred — and they pitted those passions against the "interests": security, well-being, success. Interests are also desires, but they are more survival-oriented. The Founding Fathers intended for human passions to be overruled by human interests. So people may be right when they say, "All America wants is to make the world safe for money." But consider the alternative, that is, if America had been out to serve its citizens' passions rather than their interests.

America's always had bad presidents, corrupt Congresses, and the greed and bribery that inevitably go with public office. This is nothing new. The question is not whether we're going to have corruption; the question is how much we can bear. The most recent financial scandals have been scary because they may signal that there is more corruption in big business than we can bear. We'll have to wait and see.

You say the system protects us pretty well from the passions, but does it also protect us from our interests getting out of hand? A lot of our destruction worldwide is done in the name of the "legitimate interests" of corporations, for instance.

JN: That's an interesting question, and to start answering it we have to think about how even the passions have changed since the eighteenth century. For instance, the Founding Fathers wanted fame — but back then, fame meant being respected by honorable people for your virtue. We can safely say that this idea of fame has been lost in our time, and that the passion for fame as simple celebrity is generally out of hand now all across our culture.

On the larger question of our interests getting out of hand, I think it's too soon to say. We should never forget that our system of government is self-correcting to an extent that may not be matched by any other government in the world. That doesn't mean it won't ultimately fail, or that our interests won't get out of hand and bring ruin down upon us. I don't think there's a divine ordination that says America must succeed; advanced cultures have failed before. But I think the key to our sticking around is that we keep asking the question "What is America's freedom for?" That is, what are we defending, and what are we trying to give the world? These questions will quickly lead you to other questions: What is humanity for? What is noble within us? And how is our nobility best nurtured and defended?

My view of the myth of America is that we are supposed to be about the search for conscience. Even if the outer America is crass, tough, and contradictory, we can survive as long as we are somehow defending that all-important inner search.

You paint a portrait of Abraham Lincoln as an ordinary and am-bitious man who rose to greatness. In the twentieth century, we primarily elected ordinary men who have stayed ordinary — unless you include Jimmy Carter, who seemed to find his potential only after leaving office.

JN: I think Lincoln had the seeds of greatness before he won the presidency; he was very ambitious, yet he had an in-tegrity and presence about him that was an indication of what he would become later. I don't know of any other man who could have gone into the Civil War as a leader and come out as humbled as he did, with the critical spiritual greatness that he showed.

My favorite story about Lincoln took place when he was still a lawyer in Springfield, representing a client who was fight-ing the railroad interests. A friend approaching Lincoln's office saw a man come sailing out of the second-story window, hit the ground, get up, brush himself off, and run away. The friend rushed upstairs to ask Lincoln what had happened.

"I threw him out the window," Lincoln said.

"Why? What did he do?"

"He was a lawyer for the railroad, and he asked me to cheat. He offered me five thousand dollars, but I turned him down. Then he offered me ten thousand dollars, and I turned him down again. Finally, he offered me fifteen thousand dollars, and I threw him out the window."

The friend asked Lincoln why he had chosen that point to throw the man out, and not earlier.

"Because," Lincoln answered, "he was getting near my price."

I think it takes a great man to know when he's close to selling out, and then to joke about it. I think Lincoln certainly had some craving for power, but when he got it, he was humbled by the awesome responsibility that came with it during the Civil War.

Most Americans — certainly, most white Americans — know Frederick Douglass only as a great abolitionist. In his time, however, he must have been seen as a dangerous political agitator.

JN: In his 1852 Fourth of July speech, which I quote in my book, Douglass was merciless in his criticism of the state of the nation. Yet I was struck by his clear and strong love of America. He made it painfully clear to his listeners that Americans were forgetting who they were supposed to be. In that regard I'd equate him with Martin Luther King, Jr. Although there were many slaves who freed themselves and went on to live productive lives, none wrote about it more powerfully than Douglass did. To me, it's stunning that he's not recognized by the general population as one of the great heroes of this country.

You describe the genocide of Native Americans as "the destruction of the higher consciousness by the lower." There are many who would say that this destruction continues now on a worldwide basis, as America's materialistic popular culture travels the globe and sweeps away more traditional values wherever it goes.

JN: Yes, I think we are often a negative cultural influence. The style of modernity that we project is generally crass, materialistic, and coarse. Many of the refinements that are so necessary to humanity are disappearing from other cultures —

though sometimes it's because they want to be like America, not because we're imposing our culture on them.

That's why I say that America has to justify itself by restoring and protecting in our society the same values that these historical cultures at their best brought to the earth. America as merely a materialistic culture with superior physical force will not last long. The question is: can we project a fundamental vision of spiritual freedom that is true to our real origins, and make this vision a possibility for the world? I believe our survival as a nation depends a great deal on this. In any case, it is in this direction that we can begin to offer recompense for the crime of genocide that's such a large part of our history. What's good about America is that it has within it the possibility of reinventing itself in this way.

You write, "America must give back to the world the main thing it is taking from the world." What is it that we're taking?

JN: A way of life that allows for the entry of higher forces into the world. Human beings are meant to do more than simply live out their physical lives on this earth. They're meant to do more, even, than be good stewards of the natural environment. Humanity is meant to be a conductor of great forces, passing from above, through humankind, and back. That's what I mean by the "American soul." Our society has a unique spiritual function that is all too often forgotten.

In the Iroquois creation tale you relate in the book, there's a poignant moment when the Great Peacemaker foresees a constitutional frame-work for the Five Nations, which presages many things in our own constitution. He says the point of such a confederation will be that "thinking shall replace killing" in the conduct of human affairs. Are we making much progress in this regard?

JN: Judging by the bloodiness of the last century and how this one is starting, it certainly doesn't look as if we're getting anywhere. But unless there are communities on this earth for whom thinking actually does replace killing, we may not survive as a species.

The Bush administration characterized the terrorist attacks against America as "attacks on freedom." I wonder if they wouldn't be more accurately described as "attacks on our freedom to have a lot of stuff that the rest of the world doesn't." Are we really defending the ideal of liberty, or just our wealth and power?

JN: I think that either position is something of an exaggeration — that we're wholly noble and pure, or wholly selfish and corrupt. We always have a mixture of motives. Not all of our wealth and power is bad, for instance. Many people are drawn to this country from all over the world simply by economic opportunity, and it's good that America provides that opportunity.

Some degree of material well-being is necessary for moral and spiritual well-being. The question that's so difficult to answer is: How much material well-being do we need? If materialism becomes an addiction, leading only to more of itself, then that will obviously destroy our morality and our spirituality. But extreme poverty can do the same thing. Individuals may rise above hardship, but chronic poverty is morally destructive for a country as a whole.

Do you think the long-term effects of the September 11 terrorist attacks may be salutary in part, in the sense of helping America find or renew its soul? So far we've only gone through the stages of shock, outrage, and retribution. What needs to happen next?

JN: First of all, I don't necessarily feel that we've acted entirely out of retribution; there was also an important protective element in the military actions we've taken. There are many countries that, given our military might, would have done far worse things in our situation.

Beyond that, it is necessary for America to become much more generous toward the poor of the world; we can afford to, after all. Even many of our enemies will allow that, as individuals, Americans are fundamentally generous and goodwilled. It's corporate America that projects the greedy ethos that is so often hated around the world. We need to rediscover our natural goodwill and figure out how to bring it into our relations with other peoples.

And, of course, we need to come to a better understanding of the Middle East and Islam. The Islam of the terrorists and the fundamentalists is a relatively recent invention. Historically, Islam contains dimensions of love and compassion that are as deep as anything found in the heart of Christianity and Judaism. The Islam portrayed in the media does not in any way reflect the essence of that great teaching. We also need to realize that Islamic civilization was a dominant world culture for centuries, but in the modern era it has been reduced to secondary status. Its pride as a great culture has been deeply wounded, and that can be very dangerous.

America may be the only remaining superpower, but the

laws of nature say that for every force there is a counterforce. Now our counterforce has appeared. It may not be another nation, but something else is out there, resisting us. We need to study that resistance within ourselves. An important part of spiritual development is to understand the relationship of opposing forces. We need to develop a relatively calm and impartial appreciation of what is resisting us, and why. That would be a great step forward for our soul.

Meeting God Without Religion

THE misuses and abuses of God are legion. Even as Allah is cited as the inspiration for Islamic extremists to blow themselves up, the good Lord gets credit for prodding loopy American preachers to burn copies of the Koran. A study by Julie Exline of Case Western University revealed that up to two thirds of Americans are often "mad at God" for causing their suffering — including some degree of vexation even among some self-identified atheists and agnostics. The no-deity-for-me crowd has been especially industrious of late, led by the prolific rationalist rhetoric of Dawkins, Stenger, Harris, Dennett, and Hitchens. With all this sound and fury growing louder while signifying so little, one has to wonder if almost everybody might be missing the whole point of God.

Jacob Needleman's work WHAT IS GOD? presents his personal journey through a lifetime of attempting to recognize and actualize the reality of God for himself, encompassing his own youthful period of atheism and his mature integration of mystical Christianity and the Kabbalah with the perspectives of Kant, Kierkegaard, and Gurdjieff. Like most of Needleman's books, WHAT IS GOD? presents not only the author's thinking but also his revealing interactions with students who presented him with challenges ranging from flinty, senior-citizen godlessness to young, impassioned Christian fundamentalism. Avoiding both religiosity and righteous skepticism, Needleman makes it clear that what matters about God is not what we believe but what we *are* — or more precisely, what we are making of ourselves.

In fact, Needleman concludes that the works of God are actually up to us: "It is only in and through people, inwardly developed men and women, that God can exist and act in the world of man on earth. Bluntly speaking, the proof for the existence of God is the existence of people who are inhabited by and who manifest God.... God needs not just man, but awakened man, in order to act as God in the human world. Without this conscious energy on the earth it may not be possible for divine justice, mercy, or compassion to enter the lives of human beings."

Thus, Jacob Needleman would concur with the New Atheists that the old superdaddy God whom we've variously blamed or worshipped for all the good and evil in our world has, like Elvis, left the building. As the following conversation reveals, Needleman means to focus our most serious attention on the all-important experience of God as our own highest capacity. For if *that* God is a goner, then so are we.

This conversation is the longer, original version of an interview published in edited form by *The Sun* in January 2011.

What was your first sensation or recognition of God?

JN: I was eight years old and it was summer in Philadelphia, a very hot and muggy evening. My father was sitting out on the steps looking up at the sky, which he often did. He was a very quiet man, though sometimes explosive, and I was in awe of him, a little frightened. His silences were very strong. We were overlooking the front yard where he had planted a victory garden during WWII. There was a big area of weeds around it, which I just loved; all those bugs and living things. It was heaven to me, walking through all that nature. We were on a low-rent street in a very fine area of Philadelphia, close to the Wissahickon Creek, where some of the greatest mystical sects from Germany settled before the Revolution and established communities. Very powerful area; I didn't know it at the time.

I was just sitting there, looking up at the sky, and I was stunned by what I saw. Suddenly there seemed to be a million stars, far more than normal. The whole sky was filled, almost as if you couldn't see between them. And at that point when I was trying to figure out what was happening, my father simply said, "That's God."

Nothing else passed between us, and I wondered how he knew that I was trying to understand something. Moments like that, and other moments I had as a child in nature, were all I needed to know of God. I was not at all interested in Judaism, the religion of my family. My parents were not religious, but my grandparents were Orthodox and they often took me to the synagogue. Yet I was completely allergic to that religion and their God; my God was in the sky and the trees and the weeds.

Did your awe of your father heighten your moment with him when you were looking up at the sky?

JN: Oh, no question. He was like God to me in many ways.

He was not a highly developed spiritual man, but even with all his anxieties he had the soul of a poet; he just couldn't express it. He did have a yearning that I would call deeply spiritual.

How has your experience of God changed through the years?

JN: Sitting on the steps looking at the sky with my father, and all through my childhood and adulthood, I experienced a sense of wonder that has to do with something that's out there, touching a feeling within myself. It feels like I'm part of something bigger. Once when I was in Greece, I went into an Orthodox church where I saw the head of Christ, up on the ceiling — a giant head of Christ the Creator looking down on me. There I felt the same sense of wonder, that somehow reality or the universe had offered me a gift, and I wasn't sure how to respond to it.

In the midst of this sense of wonder, all my ordinary concerns, fears, and worries are quieted. The source or trigger for this wonder is outside: the stars, the face of Christ, the extraordinary beauty of nature, looking at a slide of blood cells. What I see out there awakens an impersonal joy within me; the experience is inside, as if it's what I really am. And what I really am is not at all what I live by usually. What I live by usually, which we can call the ego, momentarily realizes that everything it always wanted — safety, security, happiness, the ability to love and receive love — is being given to me by this other, this great thing outside me. Yet it is given to me *within.*

In this moment, the ego learns with absolute certainty that its real provider is this sense of wonder, and in that moment, the ego submits because it realizes that this great gift is not of its making. The ego hasn't done it, in other words. This experience is a 'taste' of God, and anyone can have it, without religious trappings.

For a while, I led a double life in regard to God. On the one hand, I was a religious scholar and philosopher, deeply respectful of religion, yet fundamentally disbelieving of God. On the other, I had these transcendent experiences in which the word "God" was not even involved, and I would have described them simply as "higher consciousness." At some point, these two ways of being merged; it was like the wall between them became a porous membrane. I didn't become a "believer" in God in the usual religious sense, but I recognized that my experiences of wonder were in the direction of what God is.

Please recount your early encounter with the great Zen Buddhist scholar, D. T. Suzuki.

JN: As a young person I went to Harvard intending to become a scientist, and considered myself an atheist and existentialist. On the other hand, I didn't buy the scientism of the time, the reductive scientism of the analytic philosophers who were the leading thinkers of the time, at least at Harvard. I was a rebel in that respect because I had a humanistic tinge that led me to pursue the great philosophical questions of meaning — what is good and evil, life and death? — instead of reducing everything to word problems and logical puzzles. Eventually I became a philosophy major and decided that would be my career.

So there I was, a philosophy student who was allergic to religion, including Judaism and especially Christianity. I became preoccupied with the problem of the self: What is it?

What is "myself"? I was touched by Kierkegaard, who was an extraordinarily gifted and sensitive writer, but I tried very hard to ignore the Christianity in him. A lot of existentialists did that, taking his deep psychological insights and downplaying the religious part — which means they hadn't really understood him at all. His questioning of the self was very much a part of my work, as were the writings of Heidegger and Jean-Paul Sartre. I wrote an undergraduate thesis on the problem of the self, and in my senior year became interested in Zen Buddhism through a series of essays by D.T. Suzuki, a great scholar and practicing master of the tradition. He was most responsible for bringing Zen to the attention of the West.

But Zen, at that time, was deeply incomprehensible. These days it's become so well-known in certain circles that it's hardly Zen at all; it's become a brand, like Satori perfume and all that. Many people know about the koans and make jokes about them; it's sometimes hard to recognize the original tradition anymore. When I encountered Zen, its incomprehensibility also made it irresistibly attractive: What was this thing? How could it be so irrational and yet so deep and powerful, so alive with meaning?

In 1957 I heard that Suzuki happened to be visiting New York, and I was very eager to meet him. So it was arranged, and I went to a beautiful apartment where he was staying on the Upper West Side. There was this little man with these incredible eyebrows, like batwings! And he had such a presence; he was *there* in a way I had never experienced, a real strength of being. I felt very well prepared with my question; after all, I'd written my thesis on the question of the self and gotten a high grade for it.

So I asked, "What is the self, Dr. Suzuki?" I was all prepared for our discussion, with Heidegger, Kant, Kierkegaard, Nietszche, Hegel, all this stuff in my mind backing me up.

Suzuki replied, "Who is asking the question?"

Now, in 1957, nobody spoke like that! To say I was like a deer in the headlights is an understatement; in fact I was a little angry at the question. What did he mean, *who was asking the question?* All the philosophy in my head went right out the window, and I answered, very perplexed, "I am! *I'm* asking the question."

He answered, "Show me this *I.*"

Now I was really annoyed; I was just stopped dead in my tracks. I couldn't speak anymore; I had no associations, no ideas, nothing to answer with. We were both silent for a while; he didn't go any further and I certainly couldn't. We had some trivial conversation after that, but I don't remember what it was about. I got up and left, deeply disappointed and puzzled. Shaken, really — and thank God for that.

What do you mean by Suzuki's "presence"? How do you recall your experience of that?

JN: For an experience like this, there is no easily recognized language because there's something that's not expressible with the semantic categories we're used to. We're not talking about stage presence, of course. It's not what someone says; not the words; and not charisma, even in its most positive sense. He was *there*, he had gravitas, there was a kind of stillness and quiet attentiveness that created an energized atmosphere. When you meet someone like that, or they're in a room you walk into, your attention naturally goes to him. There's an attraction that's not sexual, not egoistic, not flamboyant; there's something about the person that positively compels your attention and respect. Something innately superior, but not something that has to do with appearance or style.

Morihei Ueshiba, the founder of aikido, once said that the point of mastering that martial art was to have the capacity to enter a room and quell any conflict without using a single physical technique.

JN: Yes, that would be an aspect of presence. It means that someone emanates authority because of what he or she is, rather than what he or she does, says, or looks like.

What state did his presence and his questions throw you into? You had intellectually investigated the idea of the self and had all your answers at the ready, but he threw you into an unexpected experience.

JN: He put questions to me that I couldn't wrap my mind around. Had anyone else said, "Show me this 'I'," it would have been merely clever, or the beginning of an intellectual game. But his presence carried such weight that I couldn't think; I just couldn't make any sense of it. On the one hand, I felt a great respect for the man in my gut, but my mind was confounded by him. That's a very special state. The part of me that can enter philosophical discussions and play the intellectual game as well as anyone was simply not admitted into the room. Here I was in the presence of this man whom I respected not because he was smart, or widely published, or culturally important, or Japanese, but simply for his being.

And he respected me for my being, because that's what he was calling forth by his challenges. He wasn't interested in dialoguing with me at the level of the mind, at least not the mind we're so used to using — the mind of one's personality or intellectual identity.

So he was inducing in you the same experience that a Zen koan is meant to induce: to stop the mind.

JN: Yes, because to stop the mind is to touch the being of someone... to touch his or her yearning, the essential need in the human being to search for a relationship to something higher in oneself and in the world.

Do you think he was trying to demonstrate that as long as you have an idea of who you are — your ego or yourself — that you actually don't have presence?

JN: Yes, that was a big part of it. Later I realized what a gift I'd been given: a real spiritual communication. He was not going to give me an intellectual label or answer; he meant to put me in a questioning state so that I could experience something about the self — what it isn't, what it could be, and so on. Real communication is indirect: it allows one to experience something, rather than figure it out.

It sounds like your father looking at the sky and saying "That's God," pointing you toward an experience rather than explaining what you were seeing.

JN: Yes, he was, even if he didn't know what he was doing. I don't think my father thought that way, but it was an instinct he had. With Suzuki, it was his deliberate way of respecting another person's spiritual search. He wasn't going to behave like a scholar toward this young man, whom he probably felt had some real spiritual possibility. So he gave me an authentic answer, which I only realized months later, because I had been very disillusioned after that meeting. I literally woke up in the middle of the night, exclaiming, "My God! So that's what he meant!" It was my first experience of a real spiritual communication from a master.

There seem to be many such stories in spiritual literature, where the first thing a master has to tell you delivers some kind of a shock. Instead of having wisdom directly dispensed to you, you're confronted with your own lack of resources.

JN: There's an interesting question there, because if you're being confronted without a certain intention, that's one thing; being confronted with a deliberate intention behind it is another thing. I can't say for sure that what Suzuki did with me came from his skillful means; it was a brief encounter and I didn't see him again. But the encounter certainly acted on me as if he had meant to impart this lesson. In the Hindu tradition there's the idea of the *upaguru*, which means "the guru next to you." That means that anything that is happening in your life at the moment can be your teacher, if the attitude of inner work is in place. That raises the question of how to turn toward life in a way that one can always be learning, or coming into oneself.

For instance, this drinking glass sitting here is not my guru of the moment. But if I'm talking to you about how important it is to have presence, and be aware of yourself, and in the process I absent-mindedly wave my arms and knock the glass over, spilling the water or breaking the glass, then I may make myself aware of how unconsciously I'm behaving while I'm talking about being conscious! In that moment of heightened awareness,

84

then the water glass may become my *upaguru*. If I'm willing to pay attention, that is, instead of just saying, "Oops!" or "It's not my fault."

That's a minor example, but there are countless more serious instances in life where we have the opportunity to recognize whether or not we're conscious of our state.

It reminds me of a Native American shamanic practice I've experimented with called "rock seeing," in which you pick up a fist-sized rock with one relatively smooth face and stare at it until you see a picture, or recognize some kind of face, or just get a feeling from the stone that wasn't there before. Psychologists would probably say that one is projecting unconscious material onto the rock. The Native American perspective is that you're actually becoming aware of what this bit of nature has to say to you.

JN: Yes, it's the difference between projecting meaning onto a Rorschach blot, which is truly meaningless, and recognizing an inherent meaning of nature that is always there. From an indigenous perspective, nature is always speaking to us, and yearning to be heard. The typical modern reaction to nature is instead to manipulate it, or cover it over with our own artifacts. We're constantly muting the voices of nature in our lives.

But if you really pay attention to nature — that is, be present with your full attention given to it — then nature will become much, much more vivid and suffused with mind and meaning. That's why there's a timeless, universal tradition of experiencing God in nature. It's one way of recognizing that we're part of something so much greater than ourselves.

It was not long after the encounter with Suzuki that you found your-self having to teach the fundamentals of Judaism and Christianity while still considering yourself an atheist. What were your opinions of those two traditions at the time?

JN: Well, I thought of religion as, at best, good literature; symbolic and interesting maybe, but to say that any of it was true, never! I had the standard Freudian interpretation of religion as an illusion we projected onto the universe because of our psychological weaknesses. That was the most charitable view I could manage. I regarded Christianity as particularly perverse, especially the idea that it was meant to replace Judaism. I didn't see Judaism as true either, but I still resented the implications. When I'd been a freshman at Harvard, I'd had to read THE CONFESSIONS OF ST. AUGUSTINE, and I hated that book so much: all the thee's and thou's and sin and sin and sin... I just could not bear it. I forced myself to read it, and I did well in the class, but I promised myself that I'd burn the book as soon as I could. Sure enough, when the class was over, I went to the fireplace in my room and burned St. Augustine one page at a time!

Not long after, when I started teaching at San Francisco State, I was required to teach the history of Western religious thought. When I came to read St. Augustine again to prepare for the class, I found it to be a deeply beautiful book.

It makes me wonder whether any set of ideas toward which one has such a visceral negative response actually has an attraction that you don't want to recognize.

JN: I don't think so! [laughing] It's more that my initial experience with Zen Buddhism, and my encounter with Suzuki in particular, opened me up to a different way of accessing knowledge. I began reading classic works in both Judaism and Christianity that I wouldn't read, or couldn't stand to read before. It had all become fantastically interesting; why hadn't anyone told me about the wealth and depth of these traditions? Even though I was still an atheist who didn't believe these religions were true, they had become deeply interesting.

How did the experience with Suzuki enable you to read St. Augustine differently?

JN: In the beginning of my own search for deeper meaning, I recognized that from the point of view of inner being or development, I was far worse off than I thought I was. I was much farther from the state of being I would have wished to be in, or sometimes imagined that I was in. At the same time, I began to see that what was possible for me was far greater than what I had previously imagined. This dual perception would be my companion for many years. The recognition of how many illusions I entertained about myself was not discouraging, because it was paired with the knowledge that what I could be was so great. So the price of our very great potential is to see ourselves as we actually are.

This idea is at the heart of Christianity, as well as every other great spiritual tradition. It's what "sin" actually means, but I could not see that before the experience with Suzuki threw me out of my mind, as it were, and into the experience of my own being. Before, I thought that Augustine's references to sin meant that I was a bad person, and should be smacked for it. In my second reading, I could understand that he was actually echoing the paradoxical recognition of myself that was developing. At that moment, Augustine felt like my brother, my teacher, rather than my judge.

The conventional idea of sin tends to make the recognition of one's own fallibility much worse, i.e., you're not merely falling short of your potential, you're no damn good and need to confess in the hope that a superdaddy kind of God will save you. If that's not what Augustine was saying, what was his solution to the problem?

JN: Well, his solution was belief in God or Christ, but again, not in the way that we're used to thinking, and certainly not in the way that I read Augustine the first time. His solution was, in other words, the influence that one can feel from a higher level of reality. God or Christ is a force or element of higher reality that has the quality of personhood, at least in the Christian perspective. In Eastern traditions, there is no personal God in that way. At any rate, only this higher influence, however you experience it, can confront our fallibility. We can't do it on our own at the level of personality. We can't fix ourselves as we are, but we can allow ourselves to be fixed.

So self-help is doomed?

JN: Self-help is fine for getting over some hang-ups, for successfully adapting yourself to the world, even for healing relationships, up to a certain limit. But self-help isn't going to bring about the degree of transformation that a genuinely spiritual process addresses. Seeing yourself as you really are is a great healing force in itself, if you can bear it. Some people need therapists to help them bear it. But spiritual change takes place when the seer begins to change and deepen. When you're transforming the part of you that sees, you're doing spiritual work. In self-help or therapy, you're chiefly working on what you see; you're literally working on yourself. But to do spiritual work, you must invite into yourself a higher force or identity — God, Christ, the Holy Spirit, higher Self, Brahma, Atman, Buddha-nature, whatever you want to call it — and that force alters the "you" who works on yourself. It's an entirely different level of engagement.

One of the difficulties of understanding all this is that the mind can endlessly describe itself and its workings, but it can only refer to being, or point in its general direction. What you're calling "being" is inexpressible in words. It seems that Suzuki was throwing you back on the experience of your being, which is why you found yourself wordless.

JN: Yes, at the point of encountering your own being you have to stop talking. Then either you have to remain silent or start singing. If you're going to talk about being in any meaningful way, it may have to be in mythic language. Myth, in this context, is not falsehood; it's the language of the heart and mind together, and surpasses our ordinary way of expressing ourselves. Nature often speaks to us in mythic language. We tend to paper over nature with a powerful scientific language and think we've fully described it, but to look at nature only in that way is to muzzle it.

Do you think it simply requires some maturity and life experience to see through religious language to the meaning it carries?

JN: One has to treat language as one would treat a person.

Just as you have to learn to listen to what someone is really saying, you have to learn to listen to a religion. At first St. Augustine was so alien to me; the emphasis on sinfulness seemed so extreme and I couldn't get past it. The word "sin" was such a huge wall. To peek behind the wall of language does take some maturity or experience.

For instance, studying Gurdjieff made me better able to understand sin, because it's actually the idea that we are really deeply in need of help. The situation of humanity is much worse than we like to think, and yet the possibility of humanity is also greater than we can imagine. What I began to see in Augustine, later on, was that he was speaking of this helplessness, this lack within ourselves, and the need to reach toward what we can be. That's very different from the conventional moralism of sin. When I could see beyond that moralism, I could see the greatness and insight of Augustine.

When I interviewed the late John Sanford, a Jungian psychologist, he noted that a genuine encounter with one's own dark side, or shadow, is always genuinely horrifying. But it's also a necessary part of genuine growth or individuation, in Jungian terms. Is this part of the recognition that you refer to, seeing that humanity is in a far worse condition than we'd like to admit?

JN: Yes, the shadow is a big part of what we have to accept within ourselves. Everyone has a personality, and it's a necessary part of our psyche. It's not the whole story of ourselves, but it helps us function in the world. The personality is threatened by the shadow, which represents what we find undesirable in ourselves. But the personality can be educated to live with the shadow, which heals you in a certain way. It frees you from depression or suicidal thinking, to be at peace with your darker elements. Therapy can strengthen and integrate the ego so that we can function in the everyday world, and don't fall apart.

But here's another element in oneself that has to do with divinity, or the higher level of our psyche. It's one thing to accept all the elements of our mind, from which our personality is derived; it's another thing to accept our being. To put it in Christian terms, one of the great mysteries of spiritual experience is the recognition that I am loved for what I am, and forgiven. At the ordinary level of the mind, this idea may seem sentimental, mawkish, or simply unrealistic. Properly seen, it's a Christian kind of koan that stops thought, and forces us to face a big question: Why is it so difficult for us to accept total love and forgiveness? In the course of ordinary life, we can find a kind of workable acceptance of our flaws and peccadilloes, although that often involves some ignorance of our really big problems. But complete acceptance of the totality of our being is actually impossible at the level of our mind, and has to come from a higher level, from a consciousness that's both within us and far beyond us at the same time.

Since most academic philosophers do steer clear of spirituality, what changed for you that made spiritual process and practice the focus of your work?

JN: I could never let go of the great questions of life: What is God? What is the self? Who are we really, and what are we meant to do? I couldn't accept the answers of the church or even the great religious writers, but the questions haunted me anyway.

Or they wouldn't let go of me, let me put it that way. One of the turning points of my life was reading Immanuel Kant's THE CRITIQUE OF PURE REASON, a book with a reputation of being awesomely difficult, which it is. It's like holding a cathedral in your hands. While at Harvard I was sitting on the steps of the Widener Library when I opened the book for the first time, and encountered the opening sentence:

"Human reason has this peculiar fate that in one species of its knowledge it is burdened by questions which, as prescribed by the very nature of reason itself, it is not able to ignore, but which, as transcending all its powers, it is also not able to answer."

That touched me, way down in my heart: the idea that the mind is incapable of answering the deepest questions it asks. That didn't make me a believer in religion, but it made me realize that the situation I was in was profound: the situation of being unable to answer certain fundamental questions with the mind alone. Although I didn't know it at the time, I would later learn that this was the same truth expressed in Zen Buddhism, the Upanishads, and by Meister Eckhart, Gurdjieff, and Krishnamurti: the mind alone cannot answer the questions of the heart. For a long time I didn't know what to do about this situation, but just grasping that much was my turn toward the spiritual life, as opposed to conventional religion.

When I came to San Francisco, I got interested in the new religious movements that were taking root in the West. Some of them were dubious and some of them, like Zen, were very serious. Eventually I had a student who was very interested in Gurdjieff and gave me a book called OUR LIFE WITH MR. GURDJIEFF, and I took it home and started it just to please the student. The book is the autobiographical story of a composer, Thomas de Hartmann, who tells about journeying out of Russia during the Revolution with Gurdjieff. I stayed up all night reading it, and toward the end I realized that I was in a state that I had rarely been in: the book made me quiet. That may not sound like much, but I was inwardly quiet in a way that was unfamiliar. And I wasn't sure what had produced that effect. The writing was nothing special and the story, while dramatic, wasn't the real point. Somehow it just balanced me, and I realized there was something there I hadn't experienced before.

After that I re-read IN SEARCH OF THE MIRACULOUS by P.D. Ouspensky, which I'd first encountered when I was younger, and realized that I had not really understood it before. I was touched by it in a way that I hadn't earlier, when it was just intellectually interesting. To make a long story short, I decided to pursue the Gurdjieff teaching, and it's stayed with me ever since.

What is Gurdjieff's significance to religion and philosophy? Where exactly does he fit in?

JN: Gurdjieff understood, as many great teachers have, that humanity is in a bad way. He called it "sleep." He said that man lives in illusion, has lost all contact with reality, both with the world and within himself. He did not use religious or philosophical language; he used instead the more scientific terms *consciousness* and *being*. He felt that much religion had been incorporated into the sleep of mankind. As it was practiced institutionally across most of the world, such religion only served to deepen our illusions and played upon our weaknesses, just as many atheists say. For instance, he said that much religion had turned faith into a human weakness instead of a contact with deeper love, feeling, and trust.

Further, what we think of as our freedom, or free will, is an illusion in Gurdjieff's view. In fact we are heavily influenced at every moment by forces within and without that we don't see and don't understand. We have the idea that we are free to do something, but instead we are actually driven by whatever we think we have chosen to do.

Gurdjieff felt that there had to be a completely new language for the awakening process. We have to be shaken deeply to wake up; he meant to bring a shock to people, very much in the way that Buddha and Jesus brought a shock to people. He thought that a new kind of scientific and psychological language was necessary to reach the modern, sleeping mind and give it a taste of a higher state of awareness.

So he was not attempting to be a philosopher in the usual sense.

JN: No, and he had rather harsh words about most of philosophy, which he called "pouring from the empty into the void." He had many ways of confronting people with their illusions about themselves. Here's a description of his purpose in his own words: "I wish to create around myself conditions in which a man would be continually reminded of the sense and aim of his existence, by an unavoidable friction between his conscience and the automatic manifestations of his nature." That was the heart of his teaching, right there.

What is the central practice of his teaching?

JN: There is a practice that very much involves attention.

In the Gurdjieffian teaching, attention has many levels. When you say that mankind is asleep, you could equally well say he has no real attention. His attention is automatic, sometimes very dispersed or distracted, and sometimes focused, but only because of a temporary stimulus or urgent need that awakens it. Conscious, willed attention to oneself and the world is the standard by which one measures oneself in this teaching. The practice involves trying to open one's inner life to another source of attention, starting with just being aware that you're here — being present. At one level, this is indeed the practice of presence. It is possible to be more present, now, but you have to practice it, and you may need help or instruction.

This is not a form of being self-conscious that would inter-fere with your daily activities. On the contrary, it means being fully engaged with whatever you're doing at a particular moment. In a sense, it's a practice of remembering yourself at any given moment, and that's why Gurdjieff gave it the name of "self-remembering." What that means exactly is not so easy to say, but it has to do with the essence of presence: trying to be open inwardly to another quality of the self, the real "I" or the real "I am" within myself. That's what Gurdjieff meant when he said "Remember yourself always, and everywhere." And merely the attempt to do it can be transformative. It's recalling what you have always been, from the beginning of time, within yourself.

Gurdjieff didn't speak in the usual way about God. As I describe in the book, the Gurdjieff teachings point the student toward a profound experience of stillness and presence that goes in the direction of God; I wouldn't say it's the same as God, but it takes you in that direction in the way that much conventional religion generally does not. I've sensed it and I know it; there's no question about its authenticity. I didn't become a believer in God in the usual sense. But I came to be absolutely certain that something we call God exists. I came to know something that's true, even if it remains ultimately inexpressible.

Does the self-remembering practice extend to what you call the "work of listening"?

JN: In WHAT IS GOD? there's a chapter about my encounter with a very serious fundamentalist, the kind of person I used to stay away from in my classes. But I was struck by his seriousness, and his inability to accept any idea that disagreed with his literal interpretations of the Bible. I had to understand him, so I started listening to this fundamentalist in a way I once thought I'd never be able to, and responding with respect from my point of view, even as he rejected me entirely. Instead of reacting to that, I let it in — you could say that was my spiritual discipline at the moment, to let in that rejecting point of view — and as I did so I began to feel both his humanity and mine in a new way.

We eventually came toward each other, and came out with a deeper respect for the heart and mind of each other. That's not to say that either of our views changed, but that didn't matter. It was an exchange of energy between us that allowed us to relate as two human beings rather than opponents, and that was an important experience.

What do you mean by "heart" and "deep feeling"? In the book you describe some work with your classes, in which you identified hundreds of common emotions and tried to distinguish them from deep feeling.

For instance, it's not uncommon in alternative spirituality to see the term "heart-centered," but all too often this ends up meaning little more than a mawkish sentimentality, an overreaction to Western rationality or scientism.

JN: I think our experiences of real feeling are rare. By "real" I mean non-egoistic feeling, feeling that isn't an expression of the conditioned social personality. The personality has many emotions, and they have real energy, but they are not the same as, say, a sense of wonder that transcends the ego. You could also call deep feeling "objective feeling," as it were, a feeling that is beyond the normal, limited self. We all have the capacity for it, and we all experience moments of it from time to time.

Sometimes when facing the death of a loved one, we experience a grief that is non-egoistic. It may turn into fear or anger or even guilt, but at least for a while, we become truly quiet in sorrow. In that state you're a very different person; no one can annoy you, nothing is a problem. Sorrow or grief, at this level, is not a negative emotion, but a state of great sensitivity in which you know what justice and compassion really mean. It's an impartial, non-personal state of being, although it can very quickly turn into something personal. Rarely can we hold onto the deep, warm objectivity of such a feeling, but we can remember its quality largely by what it's not: it's not dogmatic, it's not stressed or tense, it's not seductive, it's not sentimental, it's not arrogant. It's a vibration that comes from the whole of something inside yourself; it has that quality of wholeness that's so much bigger than our egoistic concerns. It's "warm" because it's infused with a great compassion; it's "objective" because it's not limited to your personal, self-preserving perspective.

The deep feelings associated with God have nothing to do with personal gain or loss, with getting what you want or being disappointed that you don't, with battling or defeating your enemies, or with success or failure. Deep feelings, like that sense of wonder I described, are outside of time and beyond our daily concerns; they are impersonal and impartial yet powerfully experienced within ourselves. They connect us with a sense of joyous obligation to something that shows us why we're here, without any reference to religious rules or customs. Real love, deep joy, or genuine grief all have this transcendent quality.

Scripture often expresses deep feeling, where the writing appears to come from a non-egoistic state. You can find it in the Old and New Testaments, in the Upanishads, the Tao Te Ching, the Cloud of Unknowing... and if you can't understand or grasp it at first, then you may need to go live a little more, then come back and get it later. It can't be explained to you, any more than music can be explained to you. I can show you octaves and chords and talk about music theory, but that's not going to enable you to grasp Mozart. You can only appreciate music with your whole being; the same goes for the deep feeling that has something to do with God.

Without the experience of deep feeling that connects you to God, you're likely to suffer from a fundamental sense of meaninglessness. I've seen it countless times in the young people I've taught throughout the years. When push comes to shove and you get down to the real question of their hearts, it's always some form of "What's it all about? Why are we here, what are we doing, and is there something else we're meant to be doing?" Or: "What kind of bad joke is this?"

Every human being thinks about such questions, sooner or later, more or less often. What answers it is some form of deep feeling that shows us what meaning is, that gives us the experience of God rather than a belief in God. When you're far from that meaning and experience, you'll be depressed. What we can call "God" is what actually gives meaning to life, at the level of deep feeling.

In traditional terms, everything else, like sex, money, or power, is an "idol." Idols give you temporary gratification or distraction, but leave you with the feeling that "I'm still gonna die" or "You can't take it with you." The experience of God cures that, not by making you feel immortal, but by connecting you with what's timeless, both out there and within yourself. So the meaning of life is not words, but an experience. If you want to translate it into words go right ahead, but just remember that the words are not the experience.

The last couple of decades have shown a rapid increase in the number of people who identify themselves as "spiritual but not religious," as high as 70% among young adults, for instance. Do you think this is good news?

JN: I think that people are recognizing that something is missing in daily life *and* religion as we know it. There's a sense of lack. People need real meaning in their lives — something more and something higher, something that they can truly serve, and by that I don't mean charity or volunteering. We use the word "spiritual" to point toward something greater than ourselves, something inside and outside. We use it to point toward what really matters, because we know that so much of what preoccupies us doesn't really matter.

We're all very concerned about money, for instance — and money is very important — yet in the long run it's deeply unsatisfying as a top priority. Science is tremendously powerful in our culture, yet any good scientist knows that the more we figure out, the less we know about what's really going on. So science ends up deeply unsatisfying as well, as long as all it can do is produce more technology that enables us to do more things faster while ending up even more alienated — not to mention how often technology creates more problems than it solves.

We live in a very complicated, overly technical, over-hyped society that gives us Facebook and Twitter yet leaves us still longing for real human connection. What is real human connection, what needs to pass between us that isn't? Something more, something greater needs to pass between us, and that's what people are looking for when they seek their own "spirituality." There's something deeper in us that's not being responded to, and not being extended outward.

One thing that needs to pass between people is a higher quality of attention. That's not the same as simply paying more attention to each other; it's a transformative, conscious energy that passes between people when they genuinely listen to each other. Television has been very destructive in this regard, in that it portrays social and political debates as people shouting at each other. Everybody exercises the right to express their dogmatic beliefs at top volume, but we almost never see a model for deep, attentive listening. The value of genuinely being in each other's presence, regardless of whether we happen to agree, seems to be almost completely lost in our social discourse. That's why we get so little meaning from all our public arguments. It seems that we don't know how to facilitate genuine presence, the kind of authentic being with each other that may actually bring about real, positive change.

As a culture we're coming to face our spiritual poverty in a way that's a very important first step, as it would be for any individual seeker. We tend to look at God the way we look at our favorite football team — we want our side to win! And even the new atheists express some of that same egoistic passion; they want Science to win out over God. I'm all for scientific atheism in the sense that it encourages people to question the egoistic content of religion. But we don't need to throw out God so much as we need a new concept of God: a concept that's free of myth, superstition, and fear, and a concept that brings us into real presence with each other.

To get into a really meaningful conversation about the subject of God is the cure, I think, of the lot of the problems that face us. The point is not to refute each other or disprove beliefs, but to listen to each other. Without that, we have no possibility for community, for democracy, or for social intelligence. A good litmus test for God is whatever brings us toward peace and not war. If you're heading toward violence, you can stop talking about God because that's not where you're going. And it's tricky, because the love of something higher can indeed turn into attachment, which turns into violence. We have to develop the awareness to know when we're getting off the track. Real listening is real work; we have to be willing to let the other person in for a while, which means letting ourselves out. When that happens it transforms everything, at least for a moment.

The Need for Philosophy

As this book was going through its final edit in late 2012, the United States and the world were shocked by the mass murder of twenty young children and six adults, plus the shooter's suicide, at the Sandy Hook elementary school in Newtown, Connecticut. As our nation has done after numerous incidents of domestic terrorism and individual lunacy, we began to ask not only what preventive measures might be needed — including stronger gun control and better access to mental health care — but also what could be done about a "culture of violence" that seems always to shadow the American mythos of optimism, self-sufficiency, and success.

As I witnessed the national self-confrontation that went on in public forums from television news to Facebook, I was reminded of the opening to Jacob Needleman's book WHY CAN'T WE BE GOOD?:

> The question has taken many forms throughout the ages, but the words that cut through all the worlds and across all the epochs of human history are simply these:

Why do we not do what we know is good?

Why do we do what we hate?

It is the question we never really ask; and it is the only one that can make a difference.

For all the vast religious and ethical literature available to us today, for all the evidence of the futility of violence and hatred in our lives and in the world; for all our efforts to find the help we need; for all our yearning to be men and women capable of love, the question remains:

Why can't we be good?

The world's spiritual traditions have offered a variety of answers to this poignant inquiry, ranging from conventional Christianity's identification of "original sin" to the Buddhist diagnosis of attachment to desire. Whenever we must confront the most horrific excesses of our shadow side, however, the question takes on a renewed urgency. For a while, at least, our attention becomes focused on bettering the human condition — not only in terms of legislation, law enforcement, and social services, but also in terms of changing ourselves from the inside out. While something usually gets done on the legislative, enforcement, or social service fronts, relatively little seems to change about our inner nature.

That's not necessarily because Americans, or human beings in general, are incapable of real change from the inside out. Instead, it might optimistically be said that we are simply not in the habit of looking deeply inward on a regular basis. We go there most often when driven by depression or guilt, but neither of those negative states are conducive to the most fruitful or sustained kind of inner work. And it is sustained, positive inner work — which can also be called spiritual discipline — that can actually change human nature. It may be the only thing that does.

This book is offered both as a testament to the work of a modern spiritual pioneer and a primer on the kind of spiritual discipline that can be independently pursued without a particular religious conviction. We live in a time when more and more people are saying they feel "spiritual but not religious," but there's often very little articulation of what people are actually doing or pursuing that can be clearly identified as spiritual.

Jacob Needleman has devoted a remarkable career of teaching and writing to the idea that anyone can move toward a genuine spiritual discipline by getting in the habit of deep questioning — that is, pursuing philosophy as a way of life rather than an arcane academic study. This kind of philosophy does not exclude religion; in fact, it calls upon the greatest ideas of all the world's religions for inspiration, while not regarding any of them as an infallible or exclusive guide to truth. Neither is the philosophical way of life anti-scientific, although it does call for a broadening of the scientific point of view, and the application of rigorous empiricism to the kind of inner experiences that too many scientists regard as "irrational" or merely the errant side-effects of biochemical reactions.

Finally, this kind of philosophy doesn't ask us to retreat from everyday life into prolonged fits of navel-gazing or ascetic purity. Indeed, it's meant to be applied to the daily challenges of dealing with money, time, love, and everything else. Too often we take on everyday life without bringing the whole of our consciousness along with us. As a result, we struggle to make effective decisions, conduct business, and pursue healthy relationships with much of our "better nature" not available to help us. The real solution to our most difficult problems, as individuals and as a society, is more wisdom. As Jacob Needleman has reminded us countless times in an impressive body of work, more wisdom is as near to us as our willingness to ask honest, searching questions without the expectation of a quick or easy answer.

How can we bring a more active philosophy into our culture, so that it informs education, politics, the law, and so forth?

JN: I think there's a very important role for philosophy in our culture, especially our schools, although it may be a definition of philosophy that's not shared by most academicians. There's a kind of philosophy that you can use to win arguments or debates, and that's really a lower form — almost a desecration of philosophy. It's like an art of cleverness, in which someone who is trained in logical thought and formal debate can talk around you in circles, to the point where you give up trying to debate or communicate at all. That kind of "philosopher" could convince you of almost anything.

Real philosophy is something else. For example: some years ago I started teach a course on Ralph Waldo Emerson. I was a little concerned that the students wouldn't be able to follow his extraordinary language and ideas, but they ended up loving the experience. I asked them what ultimately made them feel so positive about Emerson, and they said that his thinking gave them hope. As we talked about what they meant by that, it became clear that it was the hope you feel when you connect with a part of yourself that your culture doesn't ordinarily encourage or even allow. It's the part that deeply yearns for truth and goodness, that longs to be part of something greater than oneself, that is, all the narrow personal concerns that we do have to address on a daily basis. It's a hope for the part of ourselves that's not necessarily concerned with practical applications. That part might even be called "useless" by some, yet it's absolutely essential for becoming a real, fully human being.

That aspect of philosophy is what I think our educational system needs, from the very beginning of children's schooling all the way through college. We need to let our young people experience the idea that a human being is someone who does more than just make a living — someone who does all the necessary things in life without ignoring the deeper, higher, and truer parts of ourselves.

Probably the most reflective work that most people ever do is in therapy, or if they get into various self-help approaches. What does a philosophical approach or spiritual practice offer that these perspectives don't?

JN: A good therapist knows his or her limitations. A therapist can help people get back on their feet, psychologically speaking, so that they're not terribly dysfunctional, or repeating the same kind of problem over and over again. You need therapy sometimes just to get through the night.

Now there are people in spiritual practices who should still be in therapy, and there are people in therapy who are trying to get something from it that can come only from spiritual practice. Many typical neuroses have to be addressed at the therapeutic level before you can begin to hear or appreciate the deeper voice of spirit, or even know what that means.

There's a story about Suzuki Roshi that addresses this issue. He was once leading a meditation session in a very cold room, and one of the students complained during a question-and-answer session about it, asking what could be done about the cold. Suzuki said, "If you're cold, be a cold Buddha... cold Buddha, hot Buddha... Buddha Buddha Buddha!" Now, to many people, that will simply make no sense. For the person in spiritual practice, he was teaching that you have to face whatever you're experiencing with no-mind, pure awareness. That's what actually transforms you. But if you're not ready for transformation — that is, you can't get your mind off the fact that you feel cold — then you may need to do something to feel warmer in the short term.

One common misunderstanding about spirituality is the quality of its highest ideals — for instance, the idea of Christian love or Buddhist compassion. Neither of these energies should be confused with the therapeutic goal of feeling good about yourself, or "I'm okay, you're okay." When it's said that Christ loves the sinner, for instance, it doesn't mean that he *likes* the sinner. In fact, he loves the sinner *severely*, which means that he thinks the sinner is a mess — corrupt, ignorant, and identified with the ego instead of spirit. So his message to the sinner is, "Come with me, and work — *work*."

That's because Christ, or the Zen master, knows the potential of the ordinary person or student. He knows the inner being that can be realized and brought forth, with enough inner work. But that deep level of "work" is going to be incomprehensible to the ordinary person who's wrapped up in his neuroses, and having trouble just functioning on the job or in his relationships.

Real spiritual work begins when you can see what you are, without pretense or compromise. The role of the master or teacher is to see and bring forth your potential, which you probably can't see on your own.

In a similar vein, does the West have an unrecognized philosophical bent that deeply influences us without our conscious awareness? We've talked previously about how some interpretations of Calvinism encouraged the "worship" of money in our culture. Are there other ideas or traditions that make us who we are, without our understanding what those ideas are exactly?

JN: I think most people have a number of illogical, inconsistent, or openly contradictory ideas in their head — stuff they've gotten from their education, but also through television and movies, things they've read or overheard, and so on. For instance, Americans like to think they believe in "freedom" — but what does that mean? The freedom to do what? What is this freedom for, really? You hear lots of ideas like that which are loosely thrown about, but which don't have much more meaning than a slogan, and that can easily be put to all kinds of uses. Obviously, the freedom to own an assault rifle is rather different than the freedom to receive equal pay for equal work. But in our culture, you'll hear the idea of "freedom" used in such wildly different ways that it doesn't really mean anything in particular.

So I don't think there's a single, overarching Western philosophy or world view. But something that hovers over the Western world, largely unrecognized or forgotten by most, is the philosophy of the Enlightenment dating to the seventeenth and eighteenth centuries. Simply put, that philosophy is a belief in the power of reason over mere belief. At an ordinary level, this may be perceived as the tendency to accept science over this or that religious faith. But at its highest level, the philosophical temperament of the Enlightenment means the capacity to step back from one's own strongest, most emotionally held beliefs and listen to another person's opinions and beliefs, for the ultimate goal of achieving impartiality.

This is what an "enlightened" person does — step back from his own beliefs and listen to other people's reasoning and beliefs. This means that one is willing to entertain doubt, which was not favored or even allowed in the more rigid religious environments of pre-Enlightenment times.

This Enlightenment attitude is, at its best, the hope of the West. It's very different from religious faith for its own sake, and it's different from passionate partisanship of any variety. It's an attitude that I would call deeply philosophical, because it represents the capacity to have an intentional relationship to your own mind. We in the West all have that potential, owing to the Enlightenment, even if it doesn't seem to be openly expressed all that often.

I don't know if most Americans think of reason as "stepping back" or entertaining doubt, though. We tend to think of reason as rationality, that is, what's common-sensical or logically correct as opposed to what's "irrational," superstitious, or emotional.

JN: What I try to do as a philosopher is to pursue the deeper questions of life, questions that are often considered unanswerable. And these questions are unanswerable if you're investigating them only in the usual way, with the logical or common-sense part of the mind. The whole or higher mind, what Plato called *nous*, can intuit a completely objective answer. But in our typical "fallen" state, we are habitually subjective, which is to say we're all wrapped up in our limited, personal view of things. To step back from our subjectivity is also to step back from our limited rationality, the answers that seem obvious and make us feel secure. It's when we come up against a big question that makes us insecure, because we don't immediately have a final answer, that we actually come alive, become more open and alert.

That's also where we can practice what I call "inner empiricism." This is a long and ancient tradition that has given us such spiritual practices as meditation. All the great ideas of our spiritual traditions came less from studying the world "out there" than from a disciplined observation of the inner life, the workings of the human psyche.

Is the whole mind a union of what we usually think of as "thoughts" and "feelings"?

JN: Well, you have to be careful with definitions. We tend to think of "thought" as being rational or logical, when there's much more to genuine thinking than that. And we usually think of "feeling" as mere emotion, which is not the whole story of feeling. Real feeling is non-egoistic; it is a source of knowing that directly apprehends reality. There's a tendency in the West to think that science is the best way in which to grasp reality, but that actually means looking at reality with only the intellect, without the input of deep feeling. Science wants to be objective, but the approach it takes is to divorce intellect from feeling — because of the popular idea that feeling is nothing more than egoistic emotion. Science has served us well in many ways, but it is not the only or the most important way to understand our reality.

One of the more toxic ideas that's floating about in popular consciousness these days is a neo-Darwinism that suggests everything humans do can be reduced to an "evolutionary" purpose — that is, that we are driven only by the need to survive as a species, and nothing else.

Yes, I've always found that idea ironic because the evolutionary "drive to survive" always fails eventually, for individuals as well as species. If it's our basic instinct, it's doomed to failure. Not to mention the fact that it limits our view of reality to this planet and its ecosystem. I don't think that the cosmos — or even just our solar system, to narrow things down a bit — is organized around a survival instinct.

JN: That's a good philosophical point. Evolutionists would have to step back from their habit of mind, which seems like such an obvious truth to them, in order to entertain a question like this. The point of philosophy is precisely to entertain the bigger, deeper questions that challenge our normal or automatic way of looking at things. It's a capacity we all have, but it seems underused in a scientific culture that values a certain kind of rationalism over any other point of view.

In the Hindu tradition, there's the idea that nature likes to play — and that it has instincts for beauty and for self-expression, as well as survival. The Hindu cosmology celebrates all the infinite colors and qualities of life, as well as multiple levels of perception, in a way that is so much more profound and enriching than the Western reductive view of nature as a system of species who are all just out for themselves: "I survive in order to survive." Is that really all there is to nature, and to the purpose of our lives? It's just one cut of reality, like taking a cross-section of a sawed-off tree and analyzing it for its history and naming all the sections of the inner core, then saying "here are the facts about this tree." What about the view and experience of the whole tree as a living thing?

There's a role for the reductive analysis of the material world, for taking things apart in order to discover their components and see how they function. But it's become too strong in our culture, too powerful as the dominant mode of perceiving reality. When you're always analyzing and reducing reality, you become incapable of looking at, sensing, and appreciating the whole of reality. That's where genuine feeling, as a deeper means of perception, comes alive. Our minds can resonate with the wholeness of things, and when they do, we see more and different kinds of evidence than the narrowly scientific habit of mind will see.

Would you say that an actively philosophical outlook helps you to know when it's best to be rational or analytical, and when it's best to respond with feeling?

JN: What you're talking about is wisdom — the capacity to know which situations require one kind of response rather than another kind. The love of wisdom is what "philosophy" actually means, and in ancient times philosophy was regarded as a way of life, not an academic discipline.

Does wisdom come only with age?

JN: No, and it doesn't invariably come with age, that's for sure. Wisdom may come with age, simply because more years of life experience give you more opportunities for disillusionment. You have more chances to learn the limitations of your own way of thinking, and mortality becomes more of an issue as you get older. So you have the opportunity to develop humility, which is a key to wisdom.

But we usually think of "disillusionment" as a painful, disappointing, or humiliating experience.

JN: And yet it's a very positive thing! In philosophy, dis-illusionment is precious because it means that you have become free from an illusion. And that means you have become more open to truth as it really is, and thus more human. The more you are free of illusions, the better you can open the mind — which includes the heart — to great ideas that evoke wonder and a sense of the higher possibilities of life. Our normal, greedy, conditioned "monkey mind" is always going after answers, trying to be clever, to fix everything, and so on. Disillusionment can bring that mind to a halt, and give it a chance to discover a new reality and help us become more intelligent, compassionate beings.

After all these years of teaching philosophy, what one thing, of all you have spoken about, would you wish to leave us with as being the most important? What one directive or truth would you most want people to grasp?

JN: I'm hesitant to promote any particular spiritual or philosophical path. But there are actually two practical methods, which can converge and enhance each other, for anyone who wants to pursue philosophical experience and spiritual development.

The first method is to find a "philosophical friend." By that I don't mean a guru, or someone who can teach you about a particular path. A philosophical friendship is among peers, and it's rooted in the study of the great unanswerable questions of our existence, the questions of the heart: Why am I here? Does God exist? Why does evil exist? Why do we suffer, and is death the end? What should we do with our lives? The aim is to explore such questions with each other, or perhaps in a small group, in a way that serves to deepen the questions without feeling the need to come up with definite answers.

Philosophical friendship is relatively rare; it's not something you see written about or recommended often. Some of us may naturally experience it with our spouses or closest confidants, but outside of some academic environments, this kind of inner exploration among friends is not something that our culture is familiar or comfortable with. People who come together to discuss the search for truth can help each other enormously, in a way that we don't get helped by therapy or by political discussions.

It often seems that our political discussions, particularly as they're conducted in broadcast media, hardly help anyone. Everyone has their sound-bites at the ready, and "debate" seems to amount to sparring with each other and trying to score rhetorical points. On radio or television, anyone who answered a question with "I don't know" and then took a thoughtful pause would be guilty of the cardinal sin of broadcast: dead air.

JN: Then we could all use a lot more dead air — or what I would call "rich silence." The true philosophical stance is one of stepping back from yourself and your opinions, in order to take an intentional relationship to your own mind. That may sound strange, but in fact it's a completely normal capacity that everyone has. But I'm often stunned, even in philosophy classes, by how many people aren't aware of this capacity.

First you have to identify your own opinions — which are much more numerous and go much deeper than people are often aware of. In fact, opinions often have people, rather than the other way around. People get so identified with their opinions that they can't even take a step away from them, even for a moment. When people are identified with their opinions so strongly, then they feel attacked if those opinions are challenged, and you see a lot of that on TV. But the philosophical stance, which we can all attain, is independent of opinions. It's the beginning of recognizing what many spiritual traditions call the "illusory self."

This stepping-back converges with the other philosophical directive that I would recommend, which is the work of listening. It's quite rare these days to encounter the person who can hear opinions which are contradictory to their own, and receive those opinions in a respectful way, without reacting immediately or, at best, waiting for an opening in which to fire back with one's own point of view.

A very useful tool is the "mirroring" technique of dialogue, which is usually directed toward solving problems of communication. But if you pursue this kind of communication without trying to fix anything, or heal a relationship, it's a wonderful exercise in the pure art of listening. When you have to restate another's point of view, and get that person's agreement that you have indeed gotten it right before expressing yourself, you are effectively stepping back from your own opinions. There's a kind of enforced pause from the habit of mostly listening to yourself, which we all have. And you're also stepping back from the habit of wanting to win arguments, which is also universal. When you can step back in this way, some remarkable and even miraculous things can happen — not just between people, but within one's own mind.

It's worth noting that this kind of dialogue doesn't feel at all natural. It requires some training and often goes better with a trained moderator. And in fact it's somewhat frightening for most people to undertake.

JN: Yes, and what's so scary about it? Recently I was teaching the method to some students, and asked for volunteers. One young woman raised her hand, but then lowered it almost immediately. I went on and led other students in the exercise, but later I asked the first young woman why she had backed off from volunteering. And she said, "I was afraid I'd lose my opinion." I wanted to shout out to the class, "*Did you hear that?* That's the most important thing you'll hear all semester!" Isn't it interesting that we can actually be afraid of losing our opinions? What does that mean, really?

One of the biggest questions of philosophy is, why can't we be good in the ways that we know we're capable of? Why do we so often do what we mean not to do, and not do what we mean to do? Or, why can't we bridge the gap between our ordinary, everyday self and our higher self? Well, I think we can — and the first plank in the bridge is this work of listening.

I would even say that listening is the first act of love between people. I don't mean "love" in a romantic or family sense, but as the mutual exchange of the energy of attention. That energy of attention is what needs to pass between people but so often doesn't, and it's completely lacking in the midst of arguing.

So when we are arguing, we're locked into our ordinary selves. Stopping to listen means that we take that step back from ourselves...

JN: Yes, and that has great value regardless of whether it ends the argument or fixes our relationships. It's the beginning of exploring the human capacity to actually be free; in the act of real listening, we are just starting to let the higher self appear. That part of our mind that can simply see and listen, without self-defense or reaction, is the Atman, the Buddha-nature, the Holy Spirit, whatever you want to call it. As we let that part of the mind grow stronger, we begin to awaken, in spiritual terms. But awakening takes time, and it takes help. An advanced teacher or a spiritual teaching can certainly provide excellent help. We can all start the process on our own, by finding philosophical friends who can share with us the love of wisdom, and committing ourselves to the work of listening.

So there are two kinds of "opening" that I'd recommend to anyone who's serious about really practicing philosophy. The first is *opening the mind to great questions and great ideas* — that is, a serious movement toward new knowledge, new understanding. The second is *opening the heart of the mind toward another human being through the work of listening.* That is, listening as a first real step toward impartial love. These two movements, toward real knowledge and real love, can become the fusion of knowledge and love. And that's precisely the definition of wisdom, the most necessary element in all of human life.

The Works of Jacob Needleman

(Original and most recent editions are cited, separated by •)

BEING-IN-THE-WORLD: *Selected Papers of Ludwig Binswanger.* Translated and with an Introduction by Jacob Needleman. New York: Basic Books, 1963 • New York: Harper and Row Torchbook, 1968, 364p. , with new Preface.

THE NEW RELIGIONS. New York, Doubleday, 1970 • Revised edition, New York, Jeremy P. Tarcher/ Penguin, 2009; with new preface to Cornerstone Edition.

RELIGION FOR A NEW GENERATION. Edited by Jacob Needleman, A. K. Bierman and James A. Gould. New York: The Macmillan Company, 1973 • Second edition with new preface, 1973

THE SWORD OF GNOSIS: *Metaphysics, Cosmology, Tradition, Symbolism.* Baltimore, Maryland: Penguin Books, Inc., 1974. • London: Arkana/Penguin, 1986, with added preface to the second edition.

A SENSE OF THE COSMOS: *The Encounter of Modern Science and Ancient Truth.* Garden City: Doubleday, 1975 • Rhinebeck, New York: Monkfish Book Publishing Company, 2003; with new Introduction and published with the subtitle, *Scientific Knowledge and Spiritual Truth.*

SACRED TRADITION AND PRESENT NEED. Edited by Jacob Needleman and Dennis Lewis. New York: Viking, 1975.

ON THE WAY TO SELF KNOWLEDGE: *Psychotherapy and the Sacred.* Edited by Jacob Needleman and Dennis Lewis. New York: Knopf, 1976.

UNDERSTANDING THE NEW RELIGIONS. Edited by Jacob Needleman and George Baker. New York: Seabury Press, 1978.

SPEAKING OF MY LIFE: *The Art of Living in the Cultural Revolution.* Edited by Jacob Needleman; preface by John Pentland. San Francisco: Harper and Row, 1979.

LOST CHRISTIANITY. Garden City: Doubleday, 1980 • New York: Jeremy P. Tarcher/Penguin, 2003, with a new preface.

SIN AND SCIENTISM. San Francisco: Robert Briggs Associates, 1985.

CONSCIOUSNESS AND TRADITION. New York: Crossroads, 1982. • Revised edition published by Arkana/Penguin, New York, 1994 under the title THE INDESTRUCTIBLE QUESTION with two new chapters added and one chapter removed.

THE HEART OF PHILOSOPHY. New York: Knopf, 1982 • New York: Jeremy P. Tarcher/Penguin, with a new preface.

THE WAY OF THE PHYSICIAN. New York: Harper and Row, 1985 • New York: Arkana/Penguin, 1992.

SORCERERS: A Novel. San Francisco: Mercury House, Inc., 1986 • London: Arkana/Penguin, 1989.

REAL PHILOSOPHY: *An Anthology of the Universal Search for Meaning.* Edited by Jacob Needleman and David Appelbaum. London: Arkana/Penguin, 1990

THE USES OF LIFE: *a conversation with Ruth H. Cooke and Jacob Needleman.* San Francisco: Far West Institute, 1990.

MONEY AND THE MEANING OF LIFE. New York: Doubleday, 1991 • Paperback edition 1994, with a new Introduction and User's Guide.

MODERN ESOTERIC SPIRITUALITY. Edited by Antoine Faivre and Jacob Needleman. 1995: Crossroad Publishing Co.

A LITTLE BOOK ON LOVE. New York: Doubleday, 1996.
• Later published and slightly revised under the title THE WISDOM OF LOVE. Sandpoint, Idaho: Morning Light Press, 2005.

TIME AND THE SOUL. New York: Doubleday, 1998 • San Francisco: Berrett-Koehler Publishers, Inc., 2003. With a new Introduction to the paperback edition and with a Foreword by John Cleese.

THE AMERICAN SOUL. New York: Jeremy P. Tarcher/Penguin, 2002 • First paperback edition, 2003.

WHY CAN'T WE BE GOOD? New York: Jeremy P. Tarcher, 2007
• First trade paperback edition, 2008.

THE ESSENTIAL MARCUS AURELIUS. Translated and Introduced by Jacob Needleman and John P. Piazza, New York: Jeremy P. Tarcher/Penguin. 2008.

THE INNER JOURNEY: *Views from the Gurdjieff Work.* Edited by Jacob Needleman. Sandpoint Idaho, Morning Light Press, 2008.

INTRODUCTION TO THE GURDJIEFF WORK. Sandpoint, Idaho: Sandpoint Press, 2009

WHAT IS GOD? New York: Jeremy P. Tarcher/Penguin, 2009 • First trade paperback edition 2011.

AN UNKNOWN WORLD: *Notes on the Meaning of the Earth.* Jeremy P. Tarcher/Penguin, 2012.

About the Interviewer

D. PATRICK MILLER is a native of Charlotte, NC who has lived most of his adult life in northern California. He began his career in journalism as an investigative reporter while also learning typography and graphic design. After a seven-year health crisis in his thirties, Miller began writing on psychological and spiritual subject matter, becoming a leading writer on the contemporary spiritual discipline known as A COURSE IN MIRACLES. He has published over 100 magazine articles in *The Sun: A Magazine of Ideas, Yoga Journal, Columbia Journalism Review, Mother Jones,* the *East Bay Express* of Oakland, CA, and many other print and online media.

After writing several books for major publishers in the 1990s, Miller founded Fearless Books in 1997 and continues to publish his own work, as well as both print and digital titles for about a dozen other authors. In 2003, he published the first edition of the best-selling title THE DISAPPEARANCE OF THE UNIVERSE by Gary Renard, now distributed by Hay House. Miller has provided literary critiques, consultations, and editing for hundreds of writers at all levels of development through Fearless Literary Services. His books include:

INSTEAD OF THERAPY: *Help Yourself Change & Change the Help You're Getting*, with Tom Rusk, M.D. Hay House, 1991.

THE POWER OF ETHICAL PERSUASION, with Tom Rusk, M.D. Viking, 1993.

A LITTLE BOOK OF FORGIVENESS: *Challenges and Meditations for Anyone with Something to Forgive*. Viking, 1994. Republished by Fearless Books in 1999 and 2004; later revised and republished as THE WAY OF FORGIVENESS.

THE BOOK OF PRACTICAL FAITH. Henry Holt, 1995. Republished by Fearless Books in 1999, 2004, and 2012.

THE COMPLETE STORY OF THE COURSE: *The History, the People, and the Controversies Behind A Course in Miracles*. Fearless Books, 1997 (out of print; later revised and republished as UNDERSTANDING A COURSE IN MIRACLES by Ten Speed Press).

NEWS OF A NEW HUMAN NATURE: *The Best Features and Interviews on the New Spirituality*. Fearless Books, 2002 (out of print).

INSTRUCTIONS OF THE SPIRIT (poetry). Fearless Books, 2004.

LOVE AFTER LIFE (a novel). Fearless Books, 2006 and 2010.

MY JOURNEY THROUGH THE PLANT WORLD: *a novel of sexual initiation*. Fearless Books, 2008.

UNDERSTANDING A COURSE IN MIRACLES: *The History, the Message, and the Legacy of a Spiritual Path for Today*. Ten Speed Press, 2008, now published by Random House.

THE WAY OF FORGIVENESS: *Letting Go, Easing Stress, and Building Strength.* Fearless Books, 2009.

LIVING WITH MIRACLES: *A Common Sense Guide to A Course in Miracles.* Tarcher/Penguin, 2011.

Acknowledgments

Publication expenses for this title were partly defrayed by advance contributions made by the readers below, who responded to an appeal posted on Indiegogo.com and the Fearless Books website. We appreciate the enthusiasm and generosity of the following Supporters:

BRIGITTE BOUTIN	COLLEEN LOEHR
BERTA CANTON	ELIZABETH MENSINK
JOHN CROTTY	PAULA MORGAN
JOHN DAVIS	JOHN PROVOST
SARA K. DUBEL	ALEX ROSHUK ESQ.
SARI FRIEDMAN	ROBERT P. SCHMIDT JR.
ROBERT KOAGEDAL	

Our thanks also go to Honora Foah, Laurie Fox, Mitch Horowitz, Sy Safransky, and Richard Smoley for assisting in the development of this project by non-financial means.

CPSIA information can be obtained at www.ICGtesting.com
Printed in the USA
LVOW11s2106010216

473182LV00001B/74/P